S0-CFD-835

God Helps Those Who Help:

A Training Guide To Helping Others

Copyright © 2001 Father Pat Berkery
All rights reserved.

ISBN

1-58898-397-8

God Helps Those Who Help:

A Training Guide To Helping Others

God bless Stank

More

— Fr Pat

Father Pat Berkery

greatunpublished.com
Title No. 397
2001

God Helps Those Who Help:

A Training Guide To Helping Others

Introduction

Malcom was your ordinary high living young executive. At 32, he seemed to have easily reached the top of the heap. He was married, with two children, a nice home in the suburbs, along with an understanding wife, an excellent job, vacations, credit cards, two sports cars and a station wagon. One morning, he came home early from his prestige job and carefully checked each room in his spacious, well kept home. Satisfied he was alone in the house, Malcom went into his bedroom, locked the door, opened the drawer of the bedside table, pulled out his Saturday night special, put it into his mouth and pulled the trigger. Within seconds, he was dead. No one found him until a week later, when the wife and young children returned from a vacation trip in the Poconos.

A sad story, yes. Unusual no. More and more cases like Malcom's are cropping up around our country. No one can tell you what went wrong. None of the experts have their fingers on the answer as to why a person who seemingly had everything to live for, just one day pulled the curtain and called it quits. One thing we do know, however. Malcom was unhappy about life. He didn't want anymore. We also can be sure he was sending out signals, but judging by his family and friends' reactions to his suicide, no one heard him. He hadn't been able to make contact to get the help sorely needed.

Irene is 67 years old. She always had a difficult life. Her childhood was during the depression years. She managed to get married and had a lot of children, just like her mother before her. She married only once, but her husband died young, leaving her the children and little else. Yet she was able to bring up her kids and give them the chances she never had. A good woman by anyone's standards, Irene goes to church, believes in God and country. Although lately she likes to be by herself, Irene is still a respected member of her community, a pillar thereof. So what does Irene end up with? A hideous cancer eating away at her. She should be gone in a short time, so the doctors tell her. She now spends her time between painful chemotherapy and a small room in her hometown. She watches cable TV. She just sits and waits. No one comes to see her. Even her relatives call only if necessary. Irene too is sending out signals, asking for help. The professionals are already doing what they can, but there are others, supposedly more needy than her. Her church is open to her on Sunday and on their terms. She tries to make mass and communion when her torn body lets her. Otherwise, she sits and stares at the screen, looking but not seeing, her eyes vacant and cold.

Tracey is only 17, but already her life is filled with pain and disillusionment. She has been on drugs, and knows all about sex and alcohol. She went that route when her parents divorced and her father walked out of her life. She sees daddy every so often, but somehow it's not the same. Her brother and older sister cannot understand her, so they don't even try. Her friends are all too busy or into their own stuff to pay attention to her. They have their own lives to live. So Tracey is handled by appointment by the professionals. They are doing their best, but it doesn't seem to be doing it for Tracey. Tracey is sending out signals too, but the lines are jammed. She goes in for rehab, then comes out clean, ready to start the same trip allover again. It's not that she doesn't want to get her life together. It's that she needs help, and she is asking for that help. No one can be sure Tracey will make it past 20. Statistics are not in her favor.

Sad stories, you are saying. But not unusual. Such stories do not even make the news anymore. We all have our problems and we try to do the best we can. There are places people can go for help, but they have to do it themselves. No one can do it for them. What you say is true, devastatingly true.

People today have problems, and society has set up stations where anyone with a desire to help himself can get the support and advice needed. There is no denying that. But one thing is also true. We cannot hear or read about the Malcoms, Irenes and Traceys without a twinge of sadness in our own hearts. Human nature is that way. We want to reach out, to do something, except we have our own problems. Moreover, what could we do, since we are not trained to help others, at least, not like the professionals. Are we our brother's keeper?

I have heard this many times. I myself felt helpless and inadequate on many occasions when faced with another's sorrow and pain. We all want to insulate ourselves, to pretend people like Malcom, Irene and Tracey exist only in the movies. But we know they are all around us, and they are all crying for help, in one way or another. We respect the professionals. We know they too are doing the best they can with the available resources of time and money. But they can't do it all.

What is that supposed to mean? Sure they can't do it all, but neither can you or I? If someone wants to kill himself, if someone wants to hurt himself or cut himself off from the rest of the world, there really isn't anything anyone can do. True. But what we are talking about are the signals that precede the disaster, the cut-off, the dizzying spin through tragedy after tragedy. People are screaming for help, more help. You and I _can_ do something about it. We can at least help the people who are close to us, the ones we love, the ones who look to us for understanding and comfort. We can really be our brother's keeper!

They say our society is completely wrapped up in itself. No one wants to get involved. That may be true. But one thing remains constant from one society to another, and that is human nature. Human nature is fundamentally kind, generous, helpful, patient, receptive, heroic. We see this all the time, despite the failings of individuals. Human nature is a constant, a bed rock, a foundation.

If you truly want a better life for yourself and those you love, a good place to start is by helping other people, especially those you know and love, sensitizing yourself so you can not only receive another's cry for help, but are willing to extend yourself, to give of yourself so other needy persons can get back on the track before they do something inhuman to themselves, like Malcom, Irene or Tracey.

You can say "but that's not my job, man", so let me ask you a question? Aren't you part of the human race? Aren't we all part of each other? Do you really and truly "love" your relatives and friends?

Isn't it true when Malcom shoots himself, he takes a part of each of us with him? And Irene sitting alone and staring vacantly ahead, isn't her loneliness yours and mine too? Can you even picture her without twisting just a bit? And Tracey, with her whole life ahead of her, what is she to you or to me? She is the promise of life, the dawn of tomorrow, but already she is trying to check out. What does that say about any of us?

Do you need to be a professional to help people? Let's put it this way. Professionals help people and they do a great job. But what kind of a degree do you need before you can smile, before you can listen, before you can go check on someone who is hurting? What diploma or certification do you require before you will reach out to someone in trouble. Let's be honest. We all have the requisites to be kind, patient, understanding, supportive and generous. We know how to do that. We make the job of the professionals that much easier and effective to the degree we help others get the help they need.

This book is about helping others, people you know or don't know, people you love or just care about or just like. What we will do is show you how to use your own native talents to make the world a better place to live. They say the best way to help yourself is by helping others, and that is always true. They say the best way to forget your own problems is by getting out there and sharing the pain and anguish of another. And that is still true. You already have what it takes to better yourself and your environment. What we will do is show you how to use what you have to the best potential.

This book will provide you a plan, a system, one that has been tried a thousand and one times, and has always delivered. You won't have to memorize or learn anything new. You'll just be yourself, and be open to learn all about human nature. This book is not about psychology, it is not therapy, nor a stroll through esoteric pathways. The book simply opens up a way to tap your own basic human kindness and sympathy, coupled with a tested formula that works.

You benefit immediately from these techniques and insights, and your whole world benefits also. What more can we say. What better way to spend our lives than helping others. This is always a virtue and as such, it can be its own reward. Go to it, go for it, and watch your life change for the better. Go ahead and be your brother's keeper because someone out there needs you!

This book is dedicated to my friends and family

CHAPTER ONE
UNDERSTANDING HUMAN NATURE

Joan came to see me late one afternoon. She was obviously distressed. Why did Megan, her only daughter, age 14, refuse to come home? In fact, why had Megan run away in the first place. Her home was a so-called dream house, her school one of the finest in the country. Megan had everything, being an only child, yet ran off with friends not even known to her parents. Joan was looking for help. She wanted answers and she wanted them right away. I was her last resort, as she had been to the police, to the school and to a special runaway agency. They had all promised to get to work instantly, but none of them could take the time to do what Joan wanted right then, i.e., unravel this mess, so she could make sense of it all.

I said Joan wanted answers. She already had answers. But she was ignoring them. She didn't trust her own answers, but needed confirmation, approval from someone else. She really wanted someone else's answers, which as we shall see, was comparable to howling at the moon. She came to me in valid pain and incredible hurt, hopeful I could make things right again, help her understand what was going on with Megan. She was giving me an impossible task as she had to others, so that confident I was against a brick wall, she could walk away and give up on other people, telling herself no one could, would or wanted to help her.

Creating the perfect impossibility is just what most people who need help do. This gets them off the hook, allowing them to blame their pain and discomfort on others. If you are serious about helping people, you want to be equipped to really help them, and that means you want to <u>understand</u> human nature for what it really is. You want to see past the games, the tricks, the impossibilities they throw at you. You want to approach the person and his problem objectively, without becoming part of the problem. You are going to want to x-ray the person, which means getting at the bones of the problem. Unless you are able to stand outside the person, outside his problem, you won't be able to help anyone especially when he attempts to ensnare you into his unhappiness.

I was able to help Joan with some very simple techniques. Before I demonstrate these to you, however, I want to talk to you about human nature, because an understanding of human nature is the key to all helping. Why is this true? Let me ask you a question. Isn't it a fact you and the person you may want to help are both human beings? As human beings, you both have the same basic nature, the same powers, the same faculties, the same fundamental goals. In other words, as human beings, you both have a lot in common and you share a wealth of aspirations and dreams. In fact, because you are so alike, you can help each other, you can sense the needs and feelings of the other.

The commonality of nature then is the basis of any effective helping program. You as helper want to realize your own goals as well as those of the person seeking your help. The more you understand who you are and how much you share with the person in need, the more fruitful any interaction, the more effective any support provided.

Most people realize they are human beings and their environment is populated with "brother" beings. But if you are really serious about helping others, you want to bring a deep understanding of humanity to your efforts, lest you end up spinning your wheels. Specificity is required, and can be easily attained by reviewing the principal features of humanity.

There are three basic principles common to human nature and therefore essential to a thorough understanding of human nature.

Let us first name them and then devote some time to exploring them in some depth. The principles are as follows: 1) <u>All men are free</u>; 2) <u>All men are responsible</u>; and finally 3) <u>Happiness is always a choice</u>.

1. All Men Are Free

Wise men through the ages define freedom as the absence of determination. That means, freedom is found where there is no essential limitation. Freedom as we know it is simply the power to choose responsibly what we want, what we know or believe is good for us without interference from any other source.

Freedom resides in the will, hence we speak of free will. The will is the elective faculty of the human. Through the will, we seek whatever we believe will bring us satisfaction, fulfillment, pleasure. In other words, the object of the will is what the philosophers call "goodness". Even when we choose a so-called moral evil, we always do so under the guise of seeking goodness. The thief steals, an act which is morally reprehensible, because in so doing, he achieves what he wants, which is money, jewels, or what have you. If he thought stolen goods were going to hurt him, harm him, then he would have no part of them, nor would any sane person.

Most of us take our freedom for granted. If our freedom is threatened, however, we would give our blood in its defense. As Americans, we rejoice in the fact we live in a free country, so much so we remind people of this fact when they oppose what we want. Freedom is a way of life for most of us, so we look with sadness at those nations where freedom is non-existent or sharply curtailed.

We exercise our freedom every day in myriad ways. We choose the clothes we wear, the food we eat, the cars we drive, the way we spend our time. No government agency forces us to wear a uniform, nor are we compelled to eat only McDonalds, stay away from beer, or avoid the beach or movies. We live our own lifestyle doing what gives us pleasure, opting for whatever has value for us. We choose our friends, we choose our hairstyle. We are aware most people in our country live the way we do, that is, they do pretty well what pleases them.

Now this may seem all quite obvious and almost silly. But if you are serious about helping others, you want to impress on your mind you are free, that you do exercise your freedom regularly. Many people whom you are going to help seemingly are not free, at least, they would like you to believe that. Once a person forgets he is always doing what he wants, life is a series of choices, one thing rather than another, then sooner or later he starts to believe he is a victim of fate or chance, so he is only free when he says he is free.

Here is an important point about freedom. We can't be free if we have no brains. What that means is without knowledge or information, there is no freedom, because we could not "know" our options or choices. A dog is not free because he doesn't understand what's out there. You can give him a choice but he will be guided by instinct rather than understanding. A tree is alive, but it is not free. It is determined by nature to behave a certain specified way, a predictable way. If we saw a tree dancing, we would know something was awry. So too, a bird will build his nest the same way, year after year, without embellishments or improvements of any kind. It doesn't know how to do better.

As a helper, you want to be aware human beings have everything necessary to make effective choices but should difficulty in choosing arise, it does not necessarily mean one is wishy washy or weak-willed. Information could be lacking, resulting in an obscuring of potential options. The statement "I just don't know what to do" is very valid, one you hear all the time. The solution, as we will see, is in gaining requisite information or increasing one's knowledge. You can never know too much since knowledge is truly power, the power to understand as much as you can about what you might want.

Another point about freedom is this: we define ourselves through our wanting. What we want is what we are, or to paraphrase another famous saying, "you are what you want". That makes sense because the goodness we see and seek is the goodness we want to add to ourselves, so we can become better and better and have more and more. Wanting is the exercise of freedom, but it is preliminary to choosing. When we want, we demonstrate we want more of life and living. When we stop wanting, we die. As long as a person is alive, he can be helped, since he can be shown something that might appeal to him.

Many people do not pay attention to their wanting, often surrendering it, preferring to live by other people's wantings. We will talk more about that later since understanding wanting is vital to helping people. Suffice it to say for the present when we surrender our wants in favor of another's, we neutralize an essential part of ourselves. Is it any wonder we become unhappy, miserable, distraught?

Freedom cannot be taken lightly, because freedom is crucial to any understanding of human nature. God made man free and He set up the world so even He cannot interfere with man's freedom. Surely God wants man to use all His gifts in the best way possible so man can benefit from them. But God doesn't condition us to always do the so-called "right" thing. We are left to our own devices. We received the talents, the powers and the opportunities to get the most out of our lives on this planet. If we fail or if we "goof", so be it. We have no one to blame but ourselves. But as long as we are alive, we can always start over. Nothing is changed, nothing is taken from us and all we ever hoped for can still become reality, if we want.

Freedom finally means we can have whatever we want as long as we are willing to do what is required. If we want to fly to Boston, we are required to take a plane. We don't have wings. If we fail at flying to Boston, it means simply we didn't really want it that bad. We chose something else. And that's all right, because we can always go some other time, if we want. If we want to become a doctor, a lawyer or a computer expert, we have to go to school and put in the time. This is what it takes, and even then, we are not sure we will get what we want. Wanting is enough, but to make it happen, something more is required, otherwise we are simply into wishful thinking.

Whatever we want is okay, as long as it's really what we want. We don't have to make excuses or check it all out. Simply wanting is enough, if it's okay with us. That is another important point to recall in helping people. Freedom is not onerous, unless we make it so, or we buy into a system of belief that so states. But then we are simply doing what we want. As a helper, you will learn to accept people's wanting for what it is, without prejudging or interposing your own biases.

An important corollary to the concept of freedom is this, namely we are always allowed. We always have permission. We do not <u>need</u> anyone else to give us permission, for we are sufficient unto ourselves. So if we make a mistake or do something we might regret, it is pointless to punish ourselves or allow others to punish us. Whatever we did, we were allowed to do and is okay. Because we are free, we are therefore free to exercise our freedom to the extent and in the manner we choose. In fact, it cannot be otherwise. Whatever we want, then, is okay and we have permission to want it. We are, in other words, allowed to be free, allowed to make mistakes, allowed to want what we want. We do not have to clear our wanting with anyone but ourselves, because it is we who are doing the wanting. It is our action, our behavior, our exercise of our will. We may make dumb moves, we may hurt ourselves or others, but that is not the point. Those we deal with later. It might have been "good" to foresee these prior to having chosen, but the fact is we may not have, and the only answer is "so what?". As a helper of persons, you will have ample opportunity to see this reality at work, and to remind the person you are helping he or she is always allowed. That usually is something we forget or never considered, and once it is brought to our attention, we find a great load lifted from our souls as guilt melts away.

2. All Men Are Responsible

One cannot talk about freedom without also touching squarely on the concept of responsibility. Responsibility is simply that act or awareness whereby we accept we are at cause, i.e., whatever we make happen is attributable to us and no one else. Responsibility is the response to our choices, the willingness to stand up for what we want and what we choose. It is saying, "Hey, I did that and no one else."

The opposite of responsibility is evasion or blaming. When we evade the reality of our freedom, we look for scapegoats attempting to project ourselves to the public as an "effect", or as a puppet. We tell ourselves and anyone who will listen we did not cause such and such, but rather, we were either forced against our will or were a victim of circumstances, bad luck or some other invisible agent. The classic example of evasion is from Genesis where our first parents, when confronted with a simple apple bite, turned on each other blaming one another, until at her wits end, Eve pointed the finger at a serpent.

Responsibility means accountability which takes place when we not only admit we are always doing what we want, i.e., what we have chosen as best for us given certain circumstances, but are even willing to accept criticism or blame, should someone else think we messed up in some way. Without freedom, there can be neither responsibility nor accountability. Beings who are not free cannot be held responsible for their behavior. So a dog that kills a child is "punished" in a sense, but no one says he could have done otherwise if he wanted. His aberration is blamed on sickness or some other outside agent. Everyone knows a killer instinct in an animal is hardly the exercise of free choice. Animals can't be responsible because they don't know the gravity or seriousness of their actions. They can be easily controlled precisely because they are neither free nor responsible. They cannot be held accountable for their behavior.

In helping people, we see a lot of irresponsibility, a lot of evasion and a lot of blaming. But we do not have to go outside of our own lives to find ample examples of the same. We all act irresponsibly at times which is okay, as long as we accept irresponsibility for what it is, i.e., pure evasion. A defensive person is generally a person who believes people are doing things to him and he is not responsible for his own life. He does not see life as a series of choices, so he is constantly trying to protect himself from other people's judgment. The responsible person does not worry about other people, he has enough to keep his own life in order, which does not mean he will not help if asked or called upon. It simply says he is not willing to surrender the responsibility and accountability his exercise of freedom naturally entails.

We are always free to do what we want as long as we are also willing to take responsibility for whatever it is we choose. We cannot have our cake and eat it too. Which means if we are free, we are responsible. No one can criticize our choices unless they admit those choices are free and undetermined. So for example, we cannot punish a criminal for his acts unless we admit he so acted freely. Hence we have in our legal system the concept of "innocence by reason of insanity", which simply means if a criminal was not able to understand and evaluate his options, he could not have acted freely and therefore cannot be held responsible.

In helping people, the consequences of accepting the concept of responsibility seem almost dramatic. At first, people are unwilling to accept responsibility for their lives, but once they understand how freedom and responsibility are inseparable, then they breathe easier and somehow seem more powerful. I remember a young mother who had three children and a husband who preferred to leave all of the child rearing to her. He seldom lifted a hand to help her, so she began to feel overwhelmed and under-appreciated. Before long, she began to take her frustrations out on her children. Luckily her signals for help were heard and she sought counsel. As she saw her life, she was simply a victim. She wasn't doing what she wanted, i.e. what she had freely chosen, taking care of three small children, surrendering her social life, tying herself down to sleepless nights and aggravating days. She certainly preferred another form of existence. But that was all besides the point. She soon accepted the reality she was actually doing what she wanted, what she was choosing to do. She had many options, but she chose not to exercise them for whatever reasons. She chose to do what she was doing. She could see that and once the insight arrived, she knew she was also at cause. No one was doing anything to her she did not allow. That one insight into personal responsibility and accountability changed her life and she soon took steps to involve her husband and others in the care and upbringing of the children instead of simply sitting around and licking her wounds.

3. Happiness is a choice

When you see a person who is unhappy, or when you are unhappy yourself, you usually imagine happiness is a "given", a state of being coming from outside of you and caused by events over which one has no control. So from early youth, we speak of people "making" me mad, getting me upset, and so on, as though we had nothing to do with our own frame of mind and our emotions. Laura was like that. When I first met her, she was in jail. She had been picked up by the police for drunken driving, and since at age 21, this was not her first offense, the authorities kept her for several days, pending arraignment and trial. She didn't ask to see me, she was told to. But since she wanted to speed up her exit from incarceration, she went along with the judge's orders. Laura was, of course, very unhappy she was in prison. She was also very unhappy about a million and one other things. As we talked, it became evident she considered herself one of your basically good persons, who just had a lot of bad luck and could not get her life in order because other people were constantly getting in her way. She drank because she wanted to forget and also so she could feel better about herself. Her home life was impeccable. She lacked for nothing as a child but she quit college because she found it too boring. She lived in a strange city and did strange things all because she was looking for the right person, as she put it, who would sweep her off her feet. Naturally, she hadn't met Mr. Wonderful when we saw her.

I couldn't get Laura to understand she was at cause, she was free and responsible and at any time she so decided, her life could change for the better. She just wanted to feel she was helpless, because in that way, she could believe nothing was her fault, and life was just picking on her. A breakthrough in our many discussions came when she promised me just for the heck of it, she would list all her choices in a given day. She took a piece of paper and wrote down, for example, "I am choosing to open my eyes, I am choosing to smile, I am choosing to put my hand down, I am choosing to get something to eat, I am choosing to make a phone call, I am choosing to ask a question, I am choosing to wear jeans instead of a dress, I am

choosing to put on a red sweater", and on and on it went. She did
this for several days and when I next met her, she was smiling and
laughing. She couldn't believe all the choices she made in a given day,
and now she was willing to look at some of the more serious choices
in her life. Just making that list every evening proved to Laura her
whole day was one continuous choice, and so even in prison, she was
able to exercise her options.

Then we talked about happiness. I want to be happy, she said to
me. So I simply replied "If you want to be happy, you do what it takes,
which means you go and just be happy." "Is it really that simple?"
"Laura", I said, "happiness is our natural state. Just as breathing
is a natural process, so too is happiness. We don't need anyone's
permission to breathe, nor do we need anyone's okay to be happy,
just our own. We can feel good as easy as we can take a breath of fresh
air."

Of course, not everyone can easily do what it takes. It requires
attention and practice to be happy regularly. So what Laura did was
to ask herself questions throughout the day, namely "What do I
want now?" And she would say, "I want to be happy, why not?" And
she would be happy. But if she had chosen unhappiness in a given
situation, she would stop herself and ask "Do I really want to be
unhappy about such and such or so and so?" Her answer would be a
resounding "No Way!" And so, she would choose to be happy.

What we are trying to say is when you reach out to help
someone, sure as shooting you will find the person believes one <u>has
to</u> be unhappy given certain unpleasant situations. If you choose to
become unhappy because you disagree with such a belief, then how
can you help? If you distance yourself from their pain and suffering,
how can you help them? But if you keep foremost in your mind this
person is actually <u>choosing</u> to be unhappy in this given moment, then
you can help them focus on what beliefs prompt them to choose
unhappiness over happiness right now. But more about that later.

Awareness happiness is a <u>choice</u> as is unhappiness helps sustain
the proper attitude in helping others. It lets you come from a position
of strength and power, so you become impervious to another's

unhappiness. Not that you are unsympathetic or uncaring, but rather you <u>know</u> no matter what problem assails your friend, he still doesn't <u>have to</u> be unhappy, and so with your help and guidance, he may want to choose to be happy. In other words, you are not caught in the quicksand of his choice, but you know what is going on and are thereby positioned to help him.

In the next chapter, we will talk about "wanting", which when understood, puts you as a helper in an extraordinary position, for you can then see the problems afflicting your friends and loved ones from an unusual viewpoint, that is, you see them as related to the exercise of freedom. That does not mean sickness, disease and other unfortunate ills to which we are all heir as humans are a result of choice. No, we are talking about behavior, what we do with our lives and the mistakes we make, which mistakes oftentimes bring us what we call "bad luck" but which we nevertheless ought to take responsibility for.

CHAPTER TWO
WANTING

We seem to spend our whole lives wanting. "I want some of these and some of those and some of those" are words learned when we were very young. As a child, we spotted a shiny, gleaming toy and cried and cried until we got it or something better. As adults, many of us haven't changed, wanting everything we see.

We learn very early in life, however, we can't always have what we want, but that doesn't keep us from trying, from pining, or from believing life has passed us by and so feeling sorry for ourselves.

There are also a lot of things which we just don't want. When asked why, we simply reply they just don't appeal to us. We are not attracted to them. So for example, we may see a dinosaur in the museum, but not many of us want to have one for a pet. We selectively choose what we want based on whether or not value is assured.

These ideas are so basic and obvious one wonders why we even mention them. But the fact is, as we have already stated, wanting is essential to understanding human nature. Why? Because wanting is at the basis of upsets and problems. If we paid attention to how human beings use their power of wanting, we could effectively help others achieve maturity and genuine happiness.

As far as wanting goes, people usually do three things: 1) they ignore it or 2) trade it for what other people want or 3) change their wanting into "needing".

Wanting is a process of man's free will. It's object is always what we perceive as good, meaning, what we believe could help us take care of ourselves. We are not referring to moral good or moral evil. All beings are per se good, which simply means they can be desired or wanted and can contribute to life. The concept of wanting depends on desirability but most people perceive what is desirable as what is good for them personally, what can serve them or what can in some way enable them to live a more fulfilling life.

We often confuse what we like with wanting. We want what we like, but we can also want what we don't like. For example, we may not like surgery; we'd prefer something else, because few people like pain. But we may choose surgery because it will keep us alive and rid us of disease. Wanting and liking or preferring are not the same and to mingle them as identical is to create problems.

Let's look now at the usual way people treat the wanting process.

1. Wanting Is Ignored

You go to a restaurant. It is crowded. You sit and sit and the waiter seems to ignore you. You start to fume. Before you know it, you are absolutely livid. How dare he! Your whole evening is spoiled. You snap at the waiter when he comes. You argue with your guests. Your night becomes a nightmare. You sit in silence and pout, until it's time to pay the check, which you do and then you leave in a huff.

What happened? Who is to blame for this fiasco? Who caused this rotten period of time? You did! You were always doing what you wanted, i.e. what you chose to do, during the entire evening, from beginning to end. Except, out of evasion and avoidance, you chose to hide your real wanting by looking for a scapegoat, blaming others for your predicament. You had plenty of options when you noticed the "bad service". You freely chose to exercise some of them, but tried to shirk your responsibility. The fact is you wanted to sit there and wait. You could have gone and spoken to the waiter or the maitre d' or the manager. You could have made a phone call. You could have gotten up from the table with your party and walked out of the place. You actually sat there measuring all your options. Yet you chose to sit, stew and make your life miserable. You were not getting what you wanted, namely service, so you figured by getting upset, you could get what you wanted more quickly and efficiently. It went something like this:

Want > Service

-no service-

Want > Upset

-still no service-

"People should give me what I want"

> More Upset

-still no service-

RESULT = severe case of depression and unhappiness

There is nothing wrong with choosing upset in these or under any other circumstances. A person ought to be honest, however, admit his choice and take the consequences. Evasion, avoidance or blaming simply tie a person to more and more unhappiness. When we are honest, admitting to ourselves life is a series of choices, we are then able to accept reality and know we are always doing what we want, i.e., what we have chosen. The fact is, right now, I am doing what I want, what serves me, what I believe is the best for me in accordance with my beliefs. Objectively speaking, I could be dead wrong. It might be better realistically to be in Miami or trying to raise more money which really is besides the point. I don't believe that, therefore I'll do what I want because I know what I want better than other people do, whether I am wrong and they are right. I am my own best expert, and as long as I'm willing to accept the consequences of my choices, I'm allowed to be wrong.

If I want others to give me what I want, getting upset with them might work, and then it might not. Besides, getting upset as a motivator is like cutting off your nose to spite your face. It is doing something unpleasant to the self. A better and more effective way of motivating others is simply to make it worth their while to give you what you want. What motivates you? Value does. So value, that is, speaking the other person's language, motivates. If you make it worth the waiter's while, he'll accommodate you. Getting upset with yourself or at him is really counterproductive. Threatening, yelling, screaming, cursing, throwing tantrums, any attempt to frighten others into letting you have your own way simply says you are quite immature, insecure, fearful and unrealistic, believing simply <u>because you want it</u>, others should give you what you want. In the world we live in, things just don't work that way. If they did, you would have to say unhappiness is the sure road to getting what you want and achieving results-just scream, rant and rave and the world is yours. Hitler thought that was so.

The reason ranting and raving are not the path to success is because what you want may not necessarily be what others want. You want the best for yourself and your loved ones. Other people want the same for themselves. Your getting what you want may not serve them. This is known as conflict. Conflicts are resolved not by ranting, raving or pushing your weight around, but rather through compromise and rational discussion.

Take the scene in the restaurant. The waiter was doing what he wanted. Perhaps he is not a very good waiter, but that's really not the point at issue. If you knew he was not a good waiter, you may have taken your business elsewhere. The fact is, what you wanted and what he wanted were in conflict. You wanted service, he wanted to continue serving some one else, a preferred customer perhaps, a big tipper, who knows. You figured, "he should" give me what I want and serve me when I want. He figured, "I don't have to do anything I don't want. It's a free country." You didn't talk his language- a tip in the pocket or whatever. You preferred to make yourself miserable and lick your wounds. The net result was you didn't get what you wanted, that is, instant service. You wrecked your night out. The waiter? He got what he wanted, and your misery meant an inconvenience he was prepared to put up with.

So what does all this mean? Very simply, if you choose to accept the fact whatever is happening in your life right now is your choice, and you are also willing to take responsibility for it, then you cut the underpinnings of unhappiness right out from your life. You won't be unhappy when you realize you are always doing what you want, i.e., what you have chosen to do. You don't have to sit and stew ever. No one is holding you hostage. Your life is not threatened. You are always free.

In order to benefit personally from the awareness of freedom, try to become aware of what you are doing as often as you can, what you are choosing. Know the present is your choice. You could always have it otherwise if you so want and when you want. You may not like your choices, but measured against your options and your values, they are the best available for you. You might like something else or want something better for yourself, and you can always have that. But does becoming unhappy ever change the picture of the now? Does it help one iota? Is it ever worth it, especially in view of how unhappiness ravages your body and mind?

Once you become aware you are always doing what you want, i.e. whatever you are doing or feeling is a genuine choice on your part, make an attempt to respect your present feelings. Trust them. Remember you are always taking care of yourself, the best you know how based on your current beliefs. Perhaps you are not doing that great a job in the opinion of others, but what do they know about you, except what you choose to tell them or hint at. They can surmise or judge, but their conclusions are simply their own creations, having existence only in <u>their</u> minds. You know yourself and you know what you want better than anyone else in the whole wide world. Give yourself credit. Don't ignore your wanting.

2. <u>Wanting Is Traded For What Others Want</u>

The tragedy of life is living for other people. That may be a shocking statement, especially in view of the nature of this book, which is designed to show people how to help others in need. Moreover, such an assertion smacks of pure selfishness. But hold your judgments for a while, and let's see what is really meant by this statement. Many people live their lives under the guise of altruism never allowing themselves to really enjoy life as it could be. They choose to do what others say they must, should or ought to do.

Such a life, lived by other people's rules and regulations, is generally fraught with problems and rank unhappiness.

Why is it unnatural and indeed tragic to live one's own life motivated by the wants of other people? Why is it not healthy to trade your wanting for what others want? Because our free will is motivated to action by what the philosophers call "bonum sui", or to put it another way, by what turns us on. Ignoring what we really want and choosing instead another person's "bonum sui" is comparable to ordering your favorite meal and then switching plates with a complete stranger. It's simply short-circuiting one's ego structure. Why bother to consider alternatives if you are going to distrust your self, your ability to discriminate, your capability to choose what can best fulfill you?

Besides being unnatural, trading what you want for what others want results in a crippling of freedom. You really kiss your own free will goodbye letting yourself become a puppet on a string. Ultimately, you find you don't even bother to consider your own wants, always pushing them into the background so you can "make" others happy by giving them what they want. Or so you believe.

All human beings generally act out of beliefs, and beliefs, therefore, are the cradles of behavior. When we realize our beliefs motivate and color our actions, then we gain a valuable insight into the concepts of self denigration and self-abandonment. When you do something because another wants that behavior, you trade your own self-knowledge for their beliefs. You may believe this is okay, but is it? Let's look closely. Say you want to achieve a certain goal in your life. You figure you could use some help getting where ever it is you want to go. So you link up with some friends or even acquaintances. Out of a desire to ultimately get what you want, you go along with what others tell you is important. You submerge your own wants in the hope some day soon it will be your turn. Before long, you are trapped. You start to realize the other guys are getting what they want, and you are not. Actually, you are, because you believe submerging your wants in a particular situation is the best way you know of taking care of yourself. When you realize no one is considering what <u>you</u> want, you begin to loathe what is happening and you choose to become depressed, unhappy and like a martyr. You feel you were taken for a ride. Why not get out? But you procrastinate, telling yourself, success might be just around the corner. Your "friends" sense you are unhappy, so they stroke you and promise you your goals, and like a fool, you continue to trust them. "The devil you know," you tell yourself, "is better than the devil you don't know." You soon find yourself in a bitter quandary, painted into a corner. What can you do? You tell yourself you made a terrible mistake. But now you know you are trapped.

You may have made a mistake, which could be all right, if you allow it. The mistake was trading your wanting for other peoples'. You trusted others to take care of you, when in fact nature created all of us in such a way we take care of number 1 first, and then others, if we sense value in so doing. These are harsh facts you know to be true, but seldom acknowledge. You knew all along, deep down inside your heart, people related to you only because of the hope of personal value. They hoped by being with you, they would get something for themselves. No one needs anyone else, so none of your friends and acquaintances really needed you. If they chose to deal with you, it's because they found you useful in terms of their own wanting. You were, in fact, helping them.

As we said, it's quite all right to make any kind of mistake. After all, your wanting is based on information, knowledge. Very often a person doesn't have all the requisite information necessary to make a proper choice, so he makes a mistake. But we are allowed to make mistakes, for to err is really human. To forgive yourself is actually divine.

Without going into specific details, how do you free yourself from an unwanted situation, one where you are going nowhere, where your friends used you for a free ride? How can you stop trading your wants for those of others? How do you go about changing a situation you find self-defeating? The first and most important step is accepting responsibility for whatever happened. Admit you made a mistake, allowing yourself your mistake. Actually, what happened was what you wanted, what you had freely chosen, a mistake perhaps, but still "your" mistake.

Why is accepting responsibility so vital? Because until you pin it all on yourself, you will stay in blame and evasion, blocking the pathway to change and renewal. Getting upset with your friends for "betraying" you is pointless. Your anger and unhappiness won't motivate them to stop using you as a rug. Know your friends will not help you unless they see some value for themselves. In fact, they want you for their own reasons to continue giving them what they want, but because you cut them off, they dropped you like a hot potato. As long as you help them get what they want, they want you.

But unless and until you believe what your friends believe, your wants will conflict. You woke up to your no-win situation when you realized you were not communicating any more with those around you. Your friends beliefs drastically differed from yours, so there was little to share anymore. You kept hoping they would see things your way, but that never happened because you were mixing apples and oranges.

Trading your wants for those of others is self-destructive. If you don't share the beliefs of others, how can you share their wants? The only way you could is by submerging your wants. Although you did deep-six your wants, you did so because you believed you were taking care of yourself the best way you knew how. But time proved you had misjudged your friends and acquaintances, thereby short-changing yourself. You know now that you were wrong, but at times, you will not admit it because you believe it is bad to be wrong, which is not true. You can always stop censuring yourself allowing yourself to be wrong.

Let's look even more closely at all of this. Isn't the core of your unhappiness the conflict between yourself and your "friends"? Didn't it all start because you mistakenly believed others would want the same things you wanted? People will even tell you they only want what you want or what is "best for you", but how can this be so if your beliefs are at cross-purposes? You want what _you_ want and other people want what _they_ want. Believing others "should" give you what you want because you gave them what they want is just unrealistic. Telling yourself it just isn't "fair" you should give so generously and get next to nothing in return is an exercise in futility.

Nothing in life is "fair". Notice winners never speak of "fairness", only losers. Others may have used you and you may have ended up empty handed, but none of this happened against your will, but with your okay. You did not get everything you wanted, but you did get some of what you wanted, because by trading your wants for those of other, you were doing what you wanted based on mistaken beliefs, namely other people believe what you believe or others "should" give you what you want because of the law of "fairness" or "shouldness".

What have we learned? First of all, never submerge your wants. Have more respect for yourself, trust yourself to know and do what is best for yourself. You are really your own best friend, and in the final analysis, you will do what you believe is best for yourself, as will everyone else. A down-home expression some find dehumanizing says it all: "Everyone watches their own rear end". We all live by the code of self-interest and as Adam Smith taught, self-interest is the mainspring of society. To deny this is to live in a dream world. No one bothers with us, unless we make it worth their while. Watch the other guy as soon as you outgrow your usefulness. He won't even know you, although he'll make it all your fault. If you can't contribute, you become a hindrance, a hazard, a burden. You do not pull your own weight, you're too petty, you are lazy, unwilling to do your share. Translated, it all says "I don't see value in you any more".

Realize also no one has to give any of us what we want. Nor will anyone serve us unless it serves them to do so. If you really want someone to give you what you want, make it worth his while. Show him what's in it for him, and what advantages he can gain thereby. No one is altruistic by nature. When you join forces with others in any way, realize no one is going to give you what you want, no one has to, no one is obliged to and no one will, especially if his beliefs are at variance with yours.

Don't be unhappy about a "losing" situation. Just take care of yourself based on what you <u>know</u> to be true for you. If getting out of a bad situation is what you want, get out. But whatever you do, let your motivations come from within you, based upon what is real for you. Don't submerge your wants because when you do, you cut off your own soul. Don't trust others before you trust yourself or instead of trusting yourself. You know what is best for you, because you know yourself best. All other people know about you is what you tell them or what they surmise.

What you may want to do is become more aware of your own wants and choices. At the end of the day, go through what you did and what behavior really expressed your deep longings and desires. Become aware of the fact you are constantly making choices, every second, every minute, every hour, every day. But most likely, if you are like most people, you do not even listen to yourself, you do not pay attention to yourself in the hope thereby, you will ingratiate yourself with others so they will take care of you, which as you know now, is a huge mistake.

3. <u>Trading Wanting For Needing</u>

Few people know the difference between "wanting" and "needing". They believe whatever they want, they have to have, they should have and it is only fair and just. Nature, mankind and God should oblige them. Wanting is never enough, so they condition their happiness on getting whatever it is they want. They tell themselves how happy they will be if and when they get what they want. For example, a mother wants her son to become a doctor, but the boy doesn't want the grind and headaches. He tries to please Mom, but he flunks out. He's free of this burden but Mom feels bad and is unhappy. Her self-worth is jarred and scarred. Wanting was not enough, so she sells her happiness in the hopes her son will feel guilty and give her what she wants. Or a person wants to marry a girl, but when she turns him down, he goes to pieces. Wanting that girl was not enough.

When we want, we do not condition our present state of

happiness upon getting or not getting what we want. When we need, we become addicted. We have to have, otherwise we choose to become unhappy. We condition our emotional well being upon getting or not getting.

To want is natural, to need is a subjective kind of thing. Needing is a lack of trust in the self. It is attributing power to the object of our desires, power not naturally resident in the object. Needing is selling ourselves short, as though we can't be what we really are without the addition of something other than ourselves. Needing doesn't assure happiness and completion, because if it did, needing would always work and we would never be unhappy.

People use the need concept to prod themselves, to motivate themselves and keep themselves on the straight and narrow, so to speak. But what a price we pay in so doing. Not only do we lose our ability to have reality on a goal, but we get in our own way, and more often than not, we find ourselves stumbling instead of hitting our targets dead on.

The fact is, when we come from happiness, we are more apt to see the possibilities involved in achieving our goals. When we are unhappy, we focus on our misfortunes. Everything looks bleak, the whole world seems against us. Things go wrong, nothing seems easy. For example, we go out to change a tire and we are in a bad mood. We can't find the jack, and when we do, we sprain our back hoisting up the car. A simple task turns into a nightmare. The changing of a tire in a bad mood becomes just more evidence the world is against us.

We never have to be in a bad mood, except when we believe unhappiness just happens to us, we are victims of hard luck simply trying to protect ourselves. The understanding of need vs. want helps us focus on the fact we don't really have to condition our happiness on getting or not getting what we want.

Surely we want to accept nature's law so we can drop the erroneous belief we need to get what we want or else. Nature says happiness is a choice, not a given. Things and people don't make us happy. Happiness is feeling good and that's a decision we make ourselves.

If we were supposed to get whatever we needed, then all we need do is stay in a perpetual bad mood, snarl, scream, live a constant tantrum. We are adult enough to know that would not work, and it seldom does. Wanting doesn't mean we are going to get what we want. What is required is we do whatever it takes. We want a new car? Then it takes money. If we have the money, all well and good. If not, that doesn't mean we have to get the car notwithstanding, simply because we want it. Other people, especially car dealers, have their wants also. Getting unhappy is not going to get us the car. We simply want to have money, pure and simple, and that's the way life works.

So it is with everything else we want. People, places and things have nothing to do with our perception of them. That view comes from our biases, our beliefs. Endowing the extraneous with the power to make us happy or unhappy is sheer irresponsibility.

The responsible person knows he needs nothing, he is the lord of the manor. So he goes after what he wants in a detached, objective manner. If he gets what he wants, all well and good. If not, he knows he didn't do what was necessary, so he either retraces his steps and starts again or he goes on to something else. He doesn't choose to go into a bad mood, nor does he blame others for his plight, because he knows the facts.

In conclusion, we now see the importance of attending to our wants. Our wants are the cry of the self- the push towards self-fulfillment. It's of no value to censure or ignore our wants, in the sense of trading them for what other people want. By becoming aware of our wants, we are better able to take care of ourselves. Focusing on what we want puts us in a better position to help others, if that's what we really want to do. And finally, we never turn our wants into needs. We avoid becoming addicted to people or things never investing them with the power to make us happy or unhappy.

If you are going to truly help people, you want to understand and operate from the awareness life is but a series of choices, free choices and any of us are really and truly doing what we've decided upon. Hold yourself responsible for your own life, and know the other person is responsible for his or her life. You'll best help another if you can get him to realize there never is anyone to blame, so there is never a need for defensiveness. We all will do better once we just choose what we really want, knowing that is the pathway to feeling good, to being truly happy.

CHAPTER THREE
THE CORRECT ATTITUDE

I f you are going to help people, you may want to look at what you bring to people who are having difficulty coping. Let me tell you about Dianne. She was a lovely woman of thirty-five, who never seemed to have a problem of any kind. She was your proverbial do-gooder, running around in a station wagon filled with laughing, screaming kids, going on picnics, to the shore, to the movies, you name it. Dianne would be at the local blood bank helping out as a Red Cross volunteer, at a zoning meeting or helping out at a church social. Dianne had boundless energy because she played your typical super-mom. She once heard there was a family living out on the fringe of town with several small children and a sick mother. The father was nowhere to be found. Dianne went out to help, of course. But the woman refused her help and even called the police. What went wrong? According to the story around town, Dianne had every good intention. But she took over for the lady. She washed the kids, cleaned the house and brought food. All of which was good. But then she started to tell the lady how to run her family, and boldly took issue with the woman on simple things like cleanliness, health care, proper nutrition and what have you. The lady finally had enough of Dianne's interference asking her to take her food, her charity and leave. Dianne was shocked. She threatened to call in the social workers and have the kids taken away. It was at this point the mother herself picked up the phone and called the police. Dianne had never learned one basic lesson about helping people — you cannot run roughshod over their feelings but rather you want to allow them their own reality, their dignity as human beings. There is such a thing as forcing yourself and your beliefs on others, belittling their way of life in the process. Few people will put up with crass interference. Dianne thought she knew what was best for this family. Objectively, she may have been right on the dime. The fact is the mother wanted to run her own life, and as long as she didn't hurt anyone in the process, as long as she was responsible, who could fault her for holding on to her dignity and freedom? Where Dianne erred was in her attitude.

So lets talk about attitude because it is the single most important factor in helping others. As we saw with Dianne, without the correct attitude, you can hurt others, rather than help them. An attitude is a set, a collection of beliefs and judgments which we bring to a perceptual situation. In other words, an attitude is the sum total of what we believe to be true. So for example, a punk rocker has a different attitude towards life than does an opera fan. Both are human beings, but the beliefs they carry around with them allow them to see the world and their environment differently. A woman who has cancer looks at the world differently than does a healthy teenage girl. Both are alive, both stand on the brink of tomorrow, but each looks at life differently because their set or core beliefs differ. You might say an attitude is the flashlight, while the beliefs housed in the flashlight are its batteries which give a strong or weak beam or none at all.

As we have already pointed out, attitude is the sum total of our beliefs, those judgments which codify our perception of reality. Let's take a closer look at belief. What is a belief anyway? A belief basically is any assent given to truth, which assent is based upon the credibility or trustworthiness of another. As such, a belief is an indirect pathway to truth. Belief implies another person is more knowledgeable than we in a situation outside our own personal experience. So for example, if we are church members, we believe in a specific religious denomination, accepting the authority of its leaders on faith. We believe because the clergy tell us, a divine institution cannot deceive. Based on that belief, we live our lives under the guidance of a specific moral code, trying to be as good a believer as we can.

Life is almost impossible without beliefs. The fact is we cannot know everything first hand. It follows we cannot <u>want</u> to know everything first hand. We accept we are required to take someone's word for some things. If we need surgery, we accept the hospital and its surgeons are skilled and competent. We believe this but if we do have doubts, we go elsewhere and/or ask for an immediate investigation of all medical credentials.

Every time we operate on a belief, however, we do take a risk. We minimize these risks by trying to get as much first hand knowledge as possible. But the fact remains, when we do not have direct, experiential knowledge of a situation, we can be duped or tricked.

Beliefs pale when compared to direct knowledge. When we really know something, no third party interposes itself between us and the reality being known. When we exercise our knowing powers, we enjoy the full range of freedom, while in belief, freedom is limited since we don't know all we can know about a situation. I can believe the doctrine on the existence of hell. My choice is not conditioned on the truth or falsity of the belief. If hell is what they claim, I want no part of it. If heaven is as good as they say, then that's where I want to go. But I have no way of checking out the truth or falsity of this belief. I can only go along with people I trust.

So belief requires trust. But knowledge requires a higher form of trust, because when we know, we trust we are not hallucinating or making things up, but really experiencing what we are experiencing. We have the answers to life's problems within us, so it is there we should seek answers, rather than opting for beliefs all the time. But more about that later.

We have talked about attitude, beliefs and knowledge. How can we be sure we will have the optimum attitude when we approach people to help them?

Once upon a time, there was a young family whose child was autistic. His name was Raun Kabril, and he was officially diagnosed as a severely infantile autistic. His parents used to help others a lot, and they even went out of their way to teach others how to be happy in life. But now they were hit hard. Could they be happy notwithstanding the "tragedy" now stalking them? They went from expert to expert, seeking a way to bring their little boy out of the darkness of autism. But everywhere they went, people shut doors on their hopes. The experts were powerless. The young man and his wife were on their own. They had been trained in a "system" called Option, wherein people are asked to confront the beliefs that fuel their unhappiness. They decided to call on their Option background and start helping Raun by examining their beliefs about autism and the resulting attitude of helplessness and cosmic despair. Before long, they started their own home program to help Raun, enlisting volunteers and friends to support them and cooperate with them. It wasn't too long before Raun shed his autistic shell and today he is a bright, sociable, happy boy.

What was the attitude this family drew from their Option training? It is summed up by the father, Barry Kaufman in a simple sentence, one that we hope you will make part of your own life. The attitude says "TO LOVE IS TO BE HAPPY WITH!"

What does that mean? Staying in the context of autism, it means because they loved little Raun, despite his disadvantage, they could accept him just as he was, disadvantages and all. With this attitude, they could come to him from a place of acceptance and trust, knowing Raun was always doing the best he could to take care of himself, based on his current beliefs. When the father or mother came in contact with Raun, they had no fears, no judgments, no expectations, no conditions. They loved Raun just the way he was. Of course, they wanted more for him, but their own happiness was not conditioned on Raun getting better or worse. They were not about to send him back to the factory because he was "damaged".

When we volunteer to help others who are in trouble or unhappy, we want to learn the Option approach so we are positioned to really bring the best of ourselves to any encounter.

What is Option? Option is a pathway to self-fulfillment as well as a powerful instrument for helping others. It is not therapy, nor is a form of pop-psychology. Option basically is a realistic attitude that allows you to relate to yourself and your environment as they actually are, thereby enabling you to bring out the best in whatever you see. As we have already indicated, Option is an attitude of acceptance, a way of knowing whereby direct knowledge is substituted for believing. In Option there are no imperatives, no judgments, no unhappiness. When you follow the Option pathway, you look at yourself and your environment as a constant invitation towards having more of the good life.

In order to facilitate gaining the Option attitude, three little questions are used to light up the constant opportunities life presents for advancement. These questions are not indictments, nor are they frivolous. Rather these questions, when asked aloud to yourself or to the person you are helping, form the basis upon which you can confront your belief system. A regular use of these questions could rid you of deadening beliefs, allowing you to listen to your own voice and trust your own insights and experience.

Whenever you are unhappy, you can be sure a belief is hiding in the woodpile. Ferreting out that belief can be difficult, but with the Option questions, not only do you get the belief into the light, but you examine it and confront it. If the belief is turning you away from your own wantings and self-interests, you may even want to toss the belief into oblivion. No matter what, it is you making the decision, you opting for what you really want in a given situation, instead of letting yourself be bullied into accepting what some one else believes is best for you.

Here are the questions:

1. What are you unhappy about?
Clarify.

2. Why are you unhappy about that?

Clarify.

3. What are you afraid would happen if you were not unhappy about that?

Clarify.

What is this about "clarify"? Clarification is necessary only when a person hides behind generalities. For example, you ask yourself "What am I unhappy about right now?" Your immediate answer might be: "my job". That doesn't help much. Clarification is in order, which suggests you give a specific example about something in your job that might be a source of anxiety etc. for you. Saying "Give me an example" is asking for clarification. Before you know it, you are stating in concrete, realistic terms, how your unhappiness on the job is being fed by your beliefs. Always, as a general rule, ask people for clarification, saying "How about a specific example of such and such".

Okay, what have we learned? Two things primarily. First, in order to help people, you want the right attitude, one of acceptance and love. Otherwise you are unable to help anyone and you could end up as part of the problem. Second, how do you achieve the optimum attitude? Through the Option method, which is a simple dialogue with the self geared towards uncovering and confronting any beliefs which may be feeding an improper attitude. You use the Option method whenever you find acceptance to be difficult or seemingly impossible.

So let's see how the proof comes out in the pudding. Let's suppose you have a close family member who is chronically depressed and out of sorts. He barks at everyone and is hardly what you'd call a "nice" person. He seems like a walking time bomb, is very negative and snarls at the slightest provocation. You love this person, so you claim, yet he is very hard to accept and you find most people in the family are beginning to isolate him. After all, who needs the aggravation and the continual negativity he generates. You try talking to him but you end up in a bitter fight. He doesn't want to hear it, so you deal with him only when you really have to. In fact, you notice every time you attempt talking to him, he misinterprets what you say, or else he accuses you of bugging him, nagging him or getting in his way. A most difficult character, and yet you claim you love him. He wasn't always such a pill.

You'd love to see him as his old self once again, for you know he seldom is happy. You want to change him, and if you could get a pill that would restore him to his old lovable self, you'd make sure he took it several times daily. How can Option help you help him?

The first place to begin is with yourself. If you are not happy, then you are a toothless saw—completely useless. You must know that by now. Having focused your attention on yourself, what do you look at? Your attitude. You say you love this person, but the fact is you do not accept him. So what kind of love is that? Is it real love or "supposed to" love? I think you will agree it is "supposed to" love, which means you feel sorry for him. You know he's hurting himself and you want to help. But he doesn't want your help. He wants you to leave him alone. You are afraid if you leave him alone, he might hurt himself or someone else. And then you'd feel guilty the rest of your life. You'd blame yourself, irrationally so, given the fact we are all responsible for whatever we do or choose not to do. Reviewing all the facts in this case, how could you begin to accept him, i.e., really love him?

Attitude is the sum total of our beliefs. What are you believing about this person? You believe he is bad for himself, for others and especially for you. You believe he "makes" you feel unhappy, because every time he is around or you are near him, he "gets" you upset. You also believe he "should" be a nicer person and he "should" behave in a more socially acceptable manner. You "need" him to be happy and you are going to stay unhappy until he gets his act together for however long that may take. You want him to change, however, your wanting that is simply not enough. You choose to become unhappy because he doesn't agree with you he "ought to" alter his behavior. In short, you have a lot of conditions, expectations and judgments about this person you purport to love.

Do you see how these beliefs are operating within and without?

By harboring, fostering and nurturing such beliefs, you create an attitude of helplessness. This person you claim to love is not allowed by you to be and choose as he will. You want to control him, to make him the way you believe he "should" be. Not only is he allowed no input into your "plans" for him, but you are angry he doesn't meet the plans, limits and guidelines you've set up for him. Guess what? Your friend has free will too. He is a responsible human as are you and I. Your attitude, however, prompts you to approach him irrationally, as though he were not created with intelligence and freedom. What you want and what he wants are opposed, are in conflict. Because you are not getting what you want as far as reforming your friend as far as your plans for him, you choose to become unhappy and judgmental, not to say self-righteous, indignant and patronizing.

There is nothing bad about your attitude, it's just your attitude, nothing more, nothing less. However, with such an attitude, you bind yourself before you start. How can you make something "better" when your starting point is the evil it is? "Better" presupposes "good". Remember good, better, best? Not bad, better, best. Acceptance means you start not from the lack of goodness, which is so-called evil, but from the level of goodness the person really is.

When you accept a person is "bad", you are judging contrary to the evidence. For there is no such thing as "bad" or "evil". They just do not exist in reality, but are housed in the mind. They are beings of the mind, created by the mind. As moral judgments, they vary from place to place, from time to time. A cow is sacred in India, but a cow in your living room is hardly a good thing. As judgments, the designation of any being as bad or evil results from individual perceptions of the being's ascribed or inherent value. So what you value is good for you, but not necessarily good for another whose set of values may be diametrically opposed to yours.

Which is all to say that your "loved one" may be a pain in your neck, but a source of joy to his mother. Acceptance is devoid of judgment, provided the person's simple "being" is of value to you. Acceptance means you want whatever is because it is, not on a scale of 1 to 10. Acceptance is rooted in reality, not in judgment, because reality exists while judgment rents out a floor upstairs.

Option says you do not <u>have to</u> be unhappy about this person to begin with. You <u>want</u> to be unhappy for some "reason" which reason is buttressed by a belief or judgment about the way things ought to be or are supposed to be. Furthermore, Option says when you are happy, you are better positioned to help another than when you are unhappy. In other words, coming from "being" is more empowering than coming from "non-being", judgment or a perception of evil. You can have more only when there is something to start with, and a judgment of "bad" or "pain in the a—" is not a realistic starting point since there is nothing there you want to increase or have more of.

The fact you are not unhappy about this person does not mean you thereby approve of his behavior or that you like how he is hurting himself. All it means is you simply accept the way he is. You get up in the morning and it is raining. You don't like rainy days. Being happy nonetheless does not mean you thereby begin to like and approve of rainy days. It just means you unshackle yourself, you free yourself to respond as you want to whatever the day brings. But it is you who are responding, instead of reacting or being a "victim" of whatever it is you are unable to change. So too with your close relative. Your being happy has to do with you, not with him or anything about him. Your being happy says you accept him for what he is, knowing any change will come about when he says so, not because you go into a fit of depression or otherwise attempt to manipulate him to give you what you want.

Happiness empowers you because happiness lets you see the options you have for motivation. We said your relative or friend would change when he wants to. That is a simple fact. What you want and what he wants do not yet converge. When you are happy, you see him as good, not evil. So your rehabilitation plan is already on solid footing since all you expect to accomplish is allowing him to increase or have more of the goodness he already is. You no longer want to "get rid" of his evil behavior, rather you want better for him, you want more for him, you want happiness for him.

Which brings us to motivation. How can you motivate him to

want what you want? Option says man moves for value, for what he prizes. Which means you have to talk his language, deal in his currency if you expect to make a difference in his life.

What does that mean? Quite simply, offering value means just that. I remember very clearly a situation I had entered as a consultant. The principals concerned were at their wits end trying to "motivate" a member of the parish to involve himself in a particular society. All their efforts up until now had met with stony refusal. The man was just not interested. I asked the "motivators" what kind of cheese they were using to entice the man to give up his valuable time merely because they thought he "should". "Cheese", they asked incredulously, what do you mean "cheese". I mean "cheese" I responded, plain, ordinary, old fashioned cheese. Then I told them how scientists used cheese to motivate research subjects, and that if they didn't use cheese, nothing happened. "But we are not animals in the lab", they retorted indignantly. "True, we are more than animals. We are human beings" I responded. "We have a free will, and we only do what we want. What we want is what we perceive as good for us. Cheese is merely the code name for what moves the will, i.e., goodness or apparent goodness."

Cheese is a pseudonym for what makes it worth our while. Cheese is value received. The people in the rectory were not offering the man cheese, and so he wouldn't bite. They thought he "should", so they cajoled, promised and threatened, but to no avail. What they wanted and what he wanted never coincided. "What is this man's cheese?", I asked them. They didn't know, nor had they ever tried to find out, which is meant they never looked at things from his point of view, only from what they felt "should" be. Here was an obvious stalemate. This man's "cheese", we ultimately discovered, was something very simple. He found value in being with other people, not simply to talk or to play cards. He loved to discuss historical themes, and he loved to do this around coffee, in a casual, home-style atmosphere. When he was assured he would have just that kind of company in the parish society, he signed up right away. He found his "cheese" and so he wanted to do what we wanted him to do.

Motivation, then, takes root when we look at a situation from the other person's point of view, not only from what we want or the way we believe things should be. Manipulation begins when we try to force our way onto others, ignoring their wants, their values, their concerns. Artful questioning, discreet observation reveal the other person's "cheese". When we offer more of what already pleases, then we are expert motivators.

Are you ready now to help your loved one? Only you can answer that question. For only you know how you really feel about him. Perhaps there is some residue of resentment towards him. Perhaps you can't even stand the sight of him. Perhaps you really want to become more clear on him, but little butterflies beat their wings against your stomach walls every time you approach him. In other words, you still are unhappy about this person even though you are telling yourself otherwise. You can't fool your body. It tells the truth despite your wishing.

Anne was like that. She had a brother who was always bothering her in the sense he never did what she thought he "should" do. Her wants and his seldom converged. But there is no law in nature saying people who love each other should have converging wants. It would be nice and it does make for calmer seas. Anne knew she could never change her brother, but she wanted to help him. I told her all about Option and she bravely gave it a whirl. But her unhappiness refused to be evicted. How could she get from her unhappiness a gift of happiness for her brother. No way. She knew that. She and I did the Option dialogue as often as we could. It always helped. But when she faced her beloved "enemy" she would revert to type. Out came the zingers, the sarcasm, the put-downs. Her brother responded in kind and all they got for their energy were more bad feelings about each other, more unhappiness.

I asked Anne if she wanted to try something. She was game. Since I was not available for Option anytime she wanted me, I suggested she contact a close friend, give her the questions and have her ask them. The questions need only a voice. Her friend was willing to be that voice. Anne met with her friend anyway on frequent occasions. They often talked on the phone. They bumped into each other almost every day, several times. Now her friend would dutifully put the three questions to Anne. First she would ask Anne "How are you feeling right now?" Then by asking all the other questions, they would uncover the belief fueling the feeling. Anne spoke to me a week later. She knew she was on to something. "Everyone should have a friend like I have", she smilingly told me. "I have hit on beliefs I never even realized I had. My friend is relentless yet so patient. Now I am doing the same thing for her."

"And how are things with your brother?" "Much, much improved. I accept him a lot more now. We have fewer fights, and when we do, I'm on the phone right away. I don't sit and stew anymore. I just know I'm responsible and I attend to it right away with my friend." Pretty soon, Anne and her friend were joined by two other friends, and they now meet once a week. Purpose? To uncover and confront beliefs. Result? They know now that happiness is only a choice away.

No one who seriously expects to help others can ignore the Option buddy system. Happiness is but a choice, yet our beliefs are encrusted. We want to dig them up and away. We want to keep the ones that serve us, and let go of those holding us back from being happy.

Before you even try to help others then, you want to put your own house in order. You want the Option attitude? Use the buddy system regularly, often and frequently. If you don't have a friend, use a relative. But whatever you do, don't sit and lick your wounds when you are unhappy. That's like holding your breath. Instead, get on the phone and dialogue. That's how happiness becomes your permanent guest.

In the next chapter, we will get down to brass tacks and discuss actual ways you can help people by using the Option method. We don't expect to cover every contingency, nor can we do more than give you examples of what others have done. But we are confident if you do these dry runs, so to speak, you will gain more certainty for the actual situations that demand your expertise.

CHAPTER FOUR

EXAMPLES OF OPTION IN USE

Cissy is only fifteen years old. She goes to a large, urban high school. She is a sophomore there. A lot of kids at the high school use drugs. Then of course there is the perennial problem of alcohol abuse among many teenagers. Cissy knows some of her close friends are heavy into alcohol or drugs, and she would like to help them. How to even bring up the subject, no less get the person involved to dwell on it for any length of time. That was Cissy's concern. She asked me how to help. Cissy knew Option and practiced it regularly with her family. She was a happy girl and knew that "can't" was a synonym for "I don't want to". Cissy really wanted to help, so I suggested we role-play and then perhaps she could come up with some approaches of her own, rather than having me point her in the direction and be her ventriloquist.

Following is one of the first sessions Cissy and I had together. She played the "druggie" and I was Cissy. Hence the initials "D" and "C".

C   "Hi, Peter, how's it going?"

D   "Hey, Cis. Real (and then he mumbled something or other; a definite clue he was high).

(Cissy asked me frantically "What happens now?") This was my clue as to attitude. How was Cissy's attitude? Remember, if one is not "in" the Option attitude of love and acceptance, then little if any movement will occur. One might as well forget it. Peter doesn't need judgment, nor does he need instruction. He could use "acceptance" and he could use "trust", the components of a loving, happy attitude. It was time for Cissy to look first at herself, get herself clear as to what she wanted, and only then, as a happy, non-judgmental friend, could she do anything for Peter. Cissy and I then went through her present unhappiness, because remember, unhappiness is really the cause of "being frantic", unsettled, afraid or what have you. What were Cissy's real beliefs, not just about Peter's condition, but drugs and all that? These beliefs could be that "Peter was such a mess right now" or "Drugs are bad, evil and wrong" or "Peter is a bad person". Perhaps these beliefs were not in the forefront of Cissy's mind right now, but then too, they could be responsible for the ambivalence she was experiencing about Peter at the moment. She wanted to help him, but then she judgmentally felt he should know better. So right then and there we went through the three questions with Cissy. Before too long, Cissy smiled. She uncovered the belief she was really upset a young person like Peter would let himself literally go to pieces. Whereas before his drug history, he was a shy, handsome, likeable boy, now he was unshaven, dirty, smelly, (all her words) and almost sub-human. How could Cissy help Peter if these were her beliefs about him? How could Cissy show Peter being happy was great when she couldn't be happy about Peter right now? Both Cissy and Peter wanted the same thing, i.e., happiness, but each took different paths, and Cissy found out to her surprise, she was selling something (happiness) that at the moment, she did not possess.

When Cissy first found out her attitude about Peter did not allow for him to be the way he was, she began to cry and berate herself. "I should know better" was her criticism. So I had to show Cissy she was "allowed", "permitted" to be the way she was, and there was no other way she was "supposed to be", unless that was what she wanted, and then she could do what was necessary to achieve that. "But", Cissy retorted, "I have studied Option for so long and I still don't have the attitude of love and acceptance". What Cissy was saying simply put was she had failed and that was bad. "Granted that is true", I said, "why are you choosing right now to be unhappy?" And after a short while, Cissy understood that no matter how she felt in the past, she could always choose to be happy right now if only she allowed herself, gave herself permission to be happy, gave herself permission to make mistakes, gave herself permission to even be unhappy about Peter.

Now we could begin to help Peter, because Cissy was coming from happiness, i.e., love and acceptance. She could suspend her judgments about Peter and his condition. She could accept him the way he was. There was no goal set by her for Peter. She realized Peter would set his own goals, when he wanted and when he cared enough to do whatever was required. What is Cissy's role then? She simply wants to help him, to support him, to let him know someone cares. She wanted to be a presence for him, and nothing more. If Peter wanted more, then she could come from a position of strength (no judgments, no expectations, no conditions) and possibly provide him with even more help. Right now, what Peter wanted from Cissy was very little, perhaps a smile, a nod of recognition, an assurance he was still alive. He didn't want to be patronized. He surely didn't want to be preached at or to. He didn't want to be told he was "bad", and least of all, he didn't want a mother hen pecking at him. Peter wanted Cissy's humanity and her love.

So back we went to role playing. Cissy was Peter and I was Cissy.

C   Hi, Peter, how are things going?
D   Okay, I guess.
C   Great, I'm happy to hear that.
D   Well, not really. But I'll manage.
C   I know you will, Peter.
D   Yeah.
C   Hey, Peter, how about walking me to my next class?
D   You serious? Look at me.

C   (Cissy grabs Peter by the hand, and tugs at him. They begin
to walk along the pathway to the science building. No one says
anything).

D   (Peter is grunting and hiding his eyes from the sun)

C   Well, here we are. Thanks Peter. Can I see you after school
today? Maybe we can have a soda or something.

D   Naw. I'm busy after school.

C   How about tomorrow?

D   I guess not. We're not into the same things, are we? (Peter
grins)

C   Well, I'll be waiting outside school. If you change your mind,
just come by.

D   Yeah. (Peter walks away).

Now Cissy is feeling bad. I could tell from her eyes. They were
cloudy, brimming again. Cissy felt she had accomplished nothing
because Cissy had a secret agenda in helping Peter. She was going
to change him. And although she protested she loved and accepted
him, she didn't admit the term "accepted" meant "so she could make
him over to her own specifications". Since Peter hadn't taken her
bait, she felt she had failed.

Option is not a school for "do-gooders". It is simply a way
of "helping" people. Sure Cissy hadn't made any great inroads into
Peter's way of life. What she had done was "contacted" him, letting
him know she was there, that she would not judge him or put him
down for being the way he was. Peter walked away for his own
reasons. Once he began to trust Cissy, he would walk towards her for
his own reasons again.

We dealt with Cissy's unhappiness. What was she afraid would
happen if she did not feel bad right now? And Cissy knew right
then her unhappiness came from her and had nothing whatsoever to
do with Peter or with the success or failure of her talk with Peter.
Once Cissy knew that, once she took responsibility for her own
unhappiness and allowed herself to fail, she was at peace with herself.
There was nothing wrong with her not achieving her secret agenda
(to make Peter over to her own canons of normalcy). She was not

"bad" for not achieving a miracle cure. She was just Cissy, wanting something and doing something about it. She was taking the first step, contacting Peter, accepting him and opening herself up to him. How he reacted to her said nothing about her, nor about her efforts. Peter walked away because he wanted to walk away. He had his own agenda and Cissy didn't fit into it right now. So what? Cissy was on the way, and maybe Peter would come back and maybe he wouldn't.

The big question I put to Cissy was "How would you feel if Peter never came back. If Peter stayed zonked out and then one day overdosed?" Until Cissy could handle that, she couldn't handle Peter, nor could she help him. Cissy told me "naturally, I'd feel terrible if that happened". Then we both knew what Cissy was saying, i.e. Peter was not all right the way he was. There was a way he "should" be, a way he "had to" be, and until that happened, happiness was just a mirage.

Back to the three questions we went. "Why does the possibility of Peter never getting better frighten you? Why are you unhappy about that possibility?" And Cissy took the questions, went with them and before long found out she wanted better for Peter. Her mistake was believing she had to be unhappy to want better for Peter. She discovered she could be happy and still want more for Peter. Being unhappy about it all contributed not one iota to the realization of her best wishes for Peter. It was more natural to accept Peter the way he was, the way he could be and going from there, work in a non-judgmental way, a happy way to bring about whatever she wanted more of for Peter.

Cissy, as well as anyone who wishes to really help others, wants to begin by trusting herself, her insights and her wanting. When we add unhappiness to our wanting, we indicate a low level of self-trust. It is like saying wanting is not enough, wanting can't do it alone. I have to attach it to a substructure of unhappiness, as though unhappiness carries, unhappiness supports, unhappiness propels, unhappiness insures. All of which we know is just not true.

Cissy may take six months before she sees a change in Peter, a willingness on his part to even discuss his problem with her, no less take any of her advice. And then again, it may take much less time to achieve a noticeable change in Peter's attitude. Option says Cissy wants to be prepared to do what it takes, and no one knows what it takes to bring another human being around from self-destructive behavior to happiness. Option again says it cannot offer Cissy a sure-fire routine, a plan, a program which will help her to help Peter. There are no five easy steps, or thirty day plan or five year plan in Option. One simply starts from within the deep recesses of one's own being, and out of the happiness therein, solutions will emerge, the right words will come.

I told Cissy she may go for five days simply giving Peter a genuine smile of happiness, never uttering a word. When Peter is ready, he will talk. When Peter wants to be helped, he will seek Cissy out. Until then, Cissy wanted to be ready when Peter called, having no judgments, no conditions, no expectations for or about Peter. If Peter never called her, that was okay too. If Peter disappeared, that said nothing about Cissy. She could not force Peter, she could not win him over to her ways simply by thinking badly of him. She could, however, show him what happiness was all about by simply being happy in and with herself. That was her strength, that was her self-imposed mission. And anytime she wanted to call it quits, she could. There was no obligation to be for Peter, unless that was what she wanted. And only when she really wanted for Peter would she be able to be there for him when he needed her. At least now he knew she was not judging him, didn't want to change him, was not against him. Cissy had, through Option, cut a trail for Peter to herself. When Peter wanted to read the signs and follow through on what he knew, Cissy would be there. And by loving and accepting Peter as he was, not as what she wished he was, Cissy was helping as no one else could. I was pleased Cissy agreed to help Peter out of happiness, rather than out of a desperate unhappy need to restore him to his prior state of boyish innocence.

Now let's look at another example of Option at work. A close friend of yours recently discovered he has cancer. He is depressed, unhappy and angry. You want to reach out and help him. But he has cut off all meaningful communication. You drop him a line and give him the old, battered "chin up" routine. Or else you send him a religious card, assuring him you will remember him in your prayers. You feel okay about his cancer, because you don't have it- he does. That is, you can still laugh, go to work, live a normal life, eat out at fine restaurants, entertain and be entertained. Life moves normally for you, but not for your friend. You feel guilty when you are with him, so you confine your contacts to the phone or to the mails. The guilt stays with you only when you think of how he got the short end, while you have been "blessed". He knows what you are thinking and feeling, and as his "friends" make themselves scarcer, his depression multiplies. You tell yourself, "Jack is so depressed, he makes me depressed. So who wants to be around depressing people?" But that little voice gnaws away at you. Jack was a friend, he needs you now more than before, and where are you? Can Option help out here?

Option is a continuum. There is a beginning, a middle and a conclusion, so to speak. The beginning is you. Helping other people starts with you, as we have pointed out so many times. The middle depends on how much of you is present, meaning how much you trust what you are, who you are and what you have as an intelligent and free person. The conclusion is whatever results from your applying the best of who you are and what you have. It is neither good, nor bad. The conclusion is just the way things turn out.

Realizing all of this, Option rules out no situations. So let's look at your friend Jack. You decide to drop in on him now that he is out of the hospital. It's been some time since the cancer was discovered. He is home most of the time now. He is supported by his family, his little children. But he is very unhappy. Chemotherapy has taken most of his hair. He wears a woolen hat, blue in fact. He has lost weight. He just doesn't look good. You are literally driven to visit with him because of guilt. When you walk in, he smiles ruefully at you and a leaden silence grips the air once you have said the acceptable, like "How's it going, Jack? Sorry, I couldn't get by sooner, but" and the words fail you. You talk to the wife, play with the dog, and check your watch, muttering you have to go. It's getting late, and besides, you can't stand anymore. Cancer really was doing Jack in, and trying to hold back the tears, you hug Jack, sensing this might be the last time you see your old friend alive. And all the way home, you cry.

Can you help Jack? I doubt it very seriously. There is just no beginning here. Unhappiness cannot breed happiness. And you are a very unhappy fellow. The place to begin helping Jack is with you. A few questions might be in order. "Do you believe cancer is bad?" "Do you feel sorry for Jack?" "If cancer were to fell Jack, how would you feel? Could you accept that?" "Granted that you feel helpless in the face of your friend's plight, how does being unhappy empower you to help him?" "Do you believe being happy in the face of all this unhappiness is sheer idiocy?" The big question of course is, "What are you afraid would happen if you were not unhappy about Jack's sickness?"

What do you know about yourself, I mean, really "know" about yourself and Jack? Don't you really know you love Jack, you want the best for him, you support him, you are concerned, you want him to get better? Aren't all these true for you? Next question- how does being unhappy prove you love Jack, you are concerned for him. When you are happy, do you stop loving Jack, supporting him, caring for him, wanting the best for him?

Another question- do you really believe cancer is bad or evil? We may not want to have cancer, but if it's analyzed, all cancer represents is a diminished state of health. It is not death. It is not non-existence. People who have had cancer can overcome it. Statistics currently abroad say more than fifty percent of all cancers are cured, actually brought to remission. So a diminished state of health can be improved and in point of fact, more often than not, is improved on a regular basis.

My suggestion is you stay away from Jack until and when you have confronted your beliefs in the whole area. Now might be the time to get yourself a phone-buddy, someone you can run your beliefs by, someone who can help you see these beliefs objectively, so you can exchange unwanted beliefs for knowledge. By that I mean trusting what you know to be true about you, Jack and cancer, instead of exchanging knowledge for unsupported beliefs. Take whatever time you need, talk as often as you want to your phone-buddy, or any in the flesh friend who will act as your "questioner". For until you have cleared up your own misgivings about what has happened to Jack, you are unable to really help him. You become part of the problem if all you bring him is your own unhappiness.

So much for the beginning. Now what about the middle. What routine or script will Option offer? None. If you are coming out of happiness, if you trust yourself and know what you are about, the script will write itself. The three questions may not come into play until later in the visit or even during subsequent visits. No matter. A happy person will always make a contribution. You know that already. We want to be around happy people, we seek them out. They are good for us. So too for your friend Jack.

Should you pretend he doesn't even have cancer? Should you mention it? Option leaves that to you. If you accept Jack without conditions, expectations or judgments, you will say about cancer whatever you want to say. You are not afraid of it, if it's not something bad for you. Ignoring Jack's illness, as though it were a bugaboo, a "not to be mentioned" is a mistake. Jack knows he has cancer. You know it. Everyone knows it. To ignore it because it is bad is a mistake. If you are happy, you will know what to say and how to say it. If you are happy, Jack will draw strength from whatever you say about whatever.

Should you ask Jack why he is unhappy, if he is unhappy? Not if you do not want to. You could ask him a simple question like "How can I help you, Jack? I really want to help you." If Jack wants you to help him, he'll let you. If he doesn't, then Option says that's okay too. You can approach it indirectly, talking about love, acceptance, strength, friendship. Don't preach, don't patronize. Simply talk, as one friend to another. If Jack wants, he'll respond in kind. When he complains, is bitter, angry or confused, your role is not to correct him. You can simply offer him another Option, one where he discovers he doesn't have to be bitter, angry, confused or unhappy ever, no matter what. You are not there to judge, to preach, nor to change Jack. Your presence, as a happy person, simply shows Jack an option he also has.

It may take several visits, it may take just one. If you are happy, Jack will want you back, and often. You lose nothing by simply "being with" Jack, letting him call the shots. You gain everything when your happiness invites Jack to be likewise. Patience, humility, self-trust, mutual trust will work the miracle you want for Jack.

And what about the conclusion? Suppose Jack dies? Have you failed? You did not ever expect to rout the cancer, did you? People who have cancer sometimes die, and even the most sophisticated medical treatment stands by helpless. If you are clear on your goals, whatever happens, happens. You went to visit Jack primarily to help him, to show him he had an Option to unhappiness. You wanted to share your attitude of love and acceptance with him. As long as you were faithful to yourself, as long as you trusted yourself and knew your own happiness as a fact, you achieved what you set out to do, that is, to help Jack. Even if you never uttered one word about why you were there, Jack knew you were his friend, and in conveying that knowledge, you helped him. He also knew when and if he wanted to tap into your happiness resource, you would be there for him. And that helped him. If he chose to be happy, you helped him immeasurably, not to say what you did for his wife and children, who instead of having a resentful, bitter, angry person to care for, now had a new and renewed father in the house.

As you can notice by this time, Option works for other people when it first works for you. When your attitude is on the mark, when you yourself are happy, you can help anyone. You may not achieve specifically what you want, but your own happiness will not thereby diminish. Acceptance and satisfaction will be yours because you come from happiness, rather than frustration, discontent, bitterness, resentment or any of the other cloaks for unhappiness.

Now let us suppose you want to help a person who is completely negative, always complaining, yet experiences no major illness, no disasters loom in their lives, but they wallow in unhappiness. Nothing is ever right, nothing is good, and nothing pleases them. How can you bring more opportunity and more happiness in their lives.

Regina was like that. She was Maureen's sister. Maureen had adopted the Option attitude of love and acceptance, but she was sorely tried by her sister's negativity. She came to me many times looking for a way to bring Regina into the "Option fold". I took Maureen to the beginning. She was having difficulty with Regina for the simple reason that Regina was not "all right" for her. She had not accepted that it was perfectly all right for Regina to be the way she was, negative, bitter, critical, unyielding, cynical. In Maureen's mind, Regina needed Option. Regina needed conversion. Only then would Maureen be happy. What was Maureen doing? She was judging Regina. Regina is "bad". She placed conditions on Regina. Regina "should" do this, Regina "should" do that. Regina would never amount to much because she was not fulfilling the conditions for happiness that Maureen stipulated. Furthermore, Maureen had expectations of Regina. Regina was "supposed to" act happy. Regina was "supposed to be positive", Regina was "supposed to" this that and the other thing.

What Maureen was actually doing was putting a lot of burdens on Regina simply to get what she (Maureen) wanted from and of Regina. Because Regina did not measure up to Maureen's profile of what a happy person "should" be, then Maureen became unhappy. Maureen had fallen into the "better than thou" trap. She had Option. Regina didn't. Regina should, otherwise Maureen was a failure.

We can't help anybody if we do not accept them, love them just as they are, without conditions, expectations or judgments. This is a basic teaching of the Option philosophy. Moreover, it is supported by experience itself, as in the case of Maureen. Specifically, Maureen did not accept Regina as Regina was in reality, with all her imperfections and so-called faults. Regina actually "needed" nothing from Maureen, but Maureen "needed" Regina to be the way Regina wanted. When Regina did not cooperate with Maureen's "grand plan" for her, Regina put herself down, questioned her Option attitude, and chose to be unhappy. Of course, the reason she was unhappy had nothing to do with her, but everything to do with her sister, Regina.

When we "need" something, we condition our happiness upon getting it or not getting it. When we want, we simply choose to go for it, and then do whatever is necessary to achieve it. Whether we succeed or don't succeed has nothing to do with our happiness. In Maureen's case, wanting was just not enough. She put herself through the wringer, just to make an Option convert.

What could Maureen do? Happiness breeds happiness, just as unhappiness breeds unhappiness. Maureen could not turn her unhappiness about Regina into happiness. That would be like trying to make a silk purse out of a sow's ear. Instead, Maureen could start at the beginning, namely with herself. If Regina rejected Option, would that be okay with Maureen? Granted that Regina chose to be unhappy, where was it written that Maureen had to be unhappy about that? Why did Maureen believe that Regina was not allowed to be unhappy, if that was her choice?

"But", Maureen would ask me, "have you ever been around a negative person? They could drive you bananas. All they do is criticize. Their whole attitude is one of aggression towards whatever they don't like. If something comes on TV, they put down the newscaster, the press, the story, the settings and on and on they go. I feel like walking out of the room, it upsets me so."

I asked Maureen simply "Granted that what you say is true, where is it written you have to be unhappy about it? What does being unhappy do to make it all more palatable, more acceptable?" Maureen had to admit unhappiness never helped, but wasn't there a way Option could be force-fed to Regina, so she would stop creating such a negative atmosphere around the house? Maureen knew Option was about freedom, about choice, about alternatives, and thereby precluded any force or suppression of freedom. She was just desperate to help Regina. What was not being said of course was Maureen was desperate to help Maureen. She was choosing to become upset over Regina's behavior. She was choosing to allow Regina to "push her buttons". Maureen couldn't get anywhere until she took responsibility for her own unhappiness. It was her creation, not Regina's. Once Maureen could say "I am choosing to be unhappy right now", then she could start helping Regina. Blaming Regina was a blind alley. Taking responsibility for one's choices was an open sesame. Blaming Regina was admitting Maureen was a puppet and Regina could pull her strings and "make" her do what she really claimed she didn't want, namely, be unhappy.

So Maureen had a lot of "stuff" going on, a lot of beliefs she would want to handle before she could "help" Regina. God helps those who help themselves and that is also true about Option. Maureen and I went through the Option dialogue and we uncovered a lot of silly beliefs, such as "People need Option", "People are not supposed to be unhappy", "Unhappiness can be transmitted like a germ from one person to another", "People should get their acts together and be happy" and so on.

Maureen stopped creating Regina unto her own image and likeness. She chose to let Regina be the way she was and allowed Regina her freedom of choice. She took off all the burdens and "oughts" from her sister, concentrating instead on her own responsibility for her own life. That didn't mean she stopped wanting more for Regina. No, she still "wanted" Regina to be happy, but now she didn't condition her own happiness on Regina's acceptance of Option. Maureen discovered that Option "gets to" others when our own happiness oozes out of our depths and into life's mainstream. Then happiness is magnetic, charming, alluring. Option works for others only when and after it works within us first!

CHAPTER FIVE

TEACHING OTHERS THE OPTION ATTITUDE

Now you want to teach your friends the Option attitude. In other words, you want to help them. At least, you want to discuss Option with someone you care about. If you yourself are happy and attitudinally on target, your goal can be accomplished. Notice we say "can be" because one cannot have certainty as to how your friend or loved one will receive your message. But it is worth a try, isn't it? There are three basic steps, if followed, can provide you with a greater degree of possibility of success. Here they are.

Anyone with the Option lifestyle can speed anyone on the pathway of the Option attitude in three ways:

1) He points out to the person he wants to help that he (the friend) is always allowed. That means there are no "can'ts", no impossibilities if one is willing to responsibly seek and gain what one wants.

2) He assures his friend or loved one there is no need to look outside of oneself for what one wants, since every human being is already positioned in a wholesome, desirable, good place and that is within himself.

3) He assures the person he want to help there is no reason to

<u>believe in evil</u> if evil means what is bad and keeps you from getting what you want.

<u>We Are Always Allowed.</u>

Allowing reality its reality is an essential step towards resolution of any problem. Going into objection, or negation, simply blinds a person so he cannot help himself because he focuses on the intolerable.

As a helping person, your task is not over once you help someone accept the reality of reality. For often enough, once past the acceptance factor, the person begins to search for scapegoats: "Who did this to me? Who is responsible? I certainly had nothing to do with it. I obviously would do nothing to hurt myself, to become unhappy." What the person in pain is saying is "I'm not <u>supposed to</u> be treated like that by anyone or anything". He believes he would not allow himself to do anything wrong or make obvious mistakes in judgment. So where did the problem come from, if not from some outside force or agent?

You want to point out the reality of responsibility now, which is truly part and parcel of real acceptance. If something unforeseen or unwanted happened to your friend, the fact remains he is not a victim, but is always at cause. For his own reasons, he trusted, believing someone else would take care of him or keep him out of harm's way. He was careless. He must now accept the consequences of his actions or inaction. He learns next time he wants to trust himself, rather than others. There is no blame or fault to be bandied about. He simply made a mistake. What's so bad about a human being making a mistake?

<u>The Self Is The Best Place To Be and To Begin</u>

You help those in pain or trouble best when you show them there is no real need to hustle for happiness. What is necessary for happiness is already given us. What we want, we can have, provided we know what we want, and how to get it. All that remains is to open ourselves to acceptance, satisfaction and self-trust. The firm starting place for true happiness is the self. So when we are ourselves, know ourselves, love ourselves and have confidence in ourselves, we are already in the best position possible for attaining happiness.

We can begin to choose happiness as a lifestyle the moment we are willing to look at ourselves and like ourselves. Often we wish we were someone else, or we had a better body, a more handsome face, or more hair. But the fact is we are the best thing that ever happened to us, and if given the chance to be someone else, we would recoil and run back to our own home base. Deep down, we like ourselves, but we often allow silly fears and doubts to obscure the truth we know to be so, that is, we are really Numero Uno. This isn't false pride, but what psychologists refer to as "good self image".

No Need To Believe In Evil

Finally, you can help others choose happiness by enabling them to realize there is no imperative for any belief in universal, natural evil. The division of all being into good and evil is Manichean in origin. St. Augustine popularized this dichotomy. Yet God, who created all, looked on His creation and said it was good.

If we look at the concept of evil, we see it is simply the absence of good. As such, evil as evil has no possibility of real existence. It has no being in and of itself, nor can it inhere as such in any other being, as does the color red, for example. In fact, absolute evil is non-being for the simple reason nature abhors an absolute vacuum.

Goodness, on the contrary, is a transcendental character of whatever exists. Goodness is the root of desirability. If something is not good in and of itself, it cannot even be desired.

Furthermore, evil is nothing but a judgment, a statement there is a lack of desirability in a particular situation. Evil for the Muslim is not necessarily evil for the Roman Catholic or Protestant. Evil for a child is not thereby evil for the adult. Evil as a judgment simply puts a not-wanted sign on being. Moralists all agree unless an aspect of goodness appears in so-called evil, evil is not even desirable.

With the fear of evil gone, goodness becomes easier to embrace. Now you concentrate your efforts on showing there are no "should's or must's" unless one personally opts for them. Anyone

can be happy even though he makes mistakes, because he knows
now he is allowed to err. He can enjoy the safe place he is and realize
under no circumstance is he ever evil, bad or whatever. Through
your own Option attitude, you have helped your friend realize all of
us are free, good and worthy human beings.

Helping Someone Admit What He Wants

A key to understanding Option and using Option effectively
in any helping process is found in the term "wanting". We have
already spoken about this, but it bears repetition at this time.
Option has to do with "wanting" since we only want because we
are free. When we have choices, options, then we can want. Were a
person not really free, he could hardly want one thing rather than
another. He would be determined in seeking his goals. What he
needed through fatalistic instinct is what he would go after.

However, you want to appreciate there can be no wanting
without knowing. We cannot exercise free choice when we do not
know we are free. The lower level of consciousness innate to the
brute animal kingdom precisely precludes freedom of choice.

Since the will is a blind faculty, it cannot discriminate. One
must have a power that can perceive the goodness of reality and
the degrees of that goodness in relationship to self. That faculty is
mind, which naturally knows truth. Knowing truth, the mind can
perceive what exists as well as the advantages or value inherent in
possessing whatever exists. The mind is the power that estimates
thereby moving the will towards whatever is desirable.

By explaining the connection between knowledge and choice,
intelligence and will, you position the person you want to help
towards the only possible utilization of freedom. When your friend
constantly judges reality as undesirable or negative, he thereby cuts
off personal self-fulfillment and aborts his exercise of free choice.

You can also show the person you are helping ignorance or not-
knowing is really okay. One can give himself permission to be truly
ignorant of what the future may hold. Unhappiness comes when one
believes he should know, he has to know, when in fact, he doesn't know.
It is better for your friend to accept and allow his ignorance rather

than punish himself by choosing unhappiness in a given situation.

The Relationship Of Wanting To Honesty

Being human and free does not imply one can have everything he wants. Therefore to become unhappy because one does not get what he wants is silly. The truth is, we can have anything we want. To realize what is wanted, to make possibility an actuality, requires one do whatever is necessary. That means submitting to requirements. Even then, one may not get what he wants, simply because no one is <u>supposed</u> to get whatever he wants. The laws of nature do not conspire to give us everything we want simply because we want it. If we were <u>supposed</u> to get whatever we wanted, then everybody would get what he wanted, and where would freedom be?

The obvious inseparable companion of "wanting" is responsibility. We can have whatever we want, that is, there is nothing in nature that says we can't. But the transition from <u>want</u> to <u>actuality</u> rests on the person. To lash out at invisible enemies when things don't go our way, or to evade and blame are sure paths to unhappiness. Life is a series of choices. Evasion and blame do not change the reality we are always free, that myriad options exist for us at any given moment.

Honesty is always the best policy when we do not get what we want. It means admitting we did not do whatever was requisite, and that's okay. Honesty means admitting one's ignorance or inability. A knowledge gap means nothing at all. If it means anything, it means we can get the necessary information or data, should we so desire.

Admitting the truth helps a person relax about himself and his behavior. The truth says your friend really doesn't want to tell another person off, or he really doesn't want to change his job and move to another state, or he really doesn't want to ask the boss for a raise, or he really doesn't want to get rid of this or that phobia just right now. And that's all right. No one <u>should</u> do anything. Especially when he doesn't <u>know</u> what to do. With an honest acceptance of one's limitations comes an awareness it is okay to admit one really doesn't know what he wants, because that is why he doesn't want it.

Honesty relieves your friend of an intolerable burden. Now he feels he no longer wants to do something about everything. This does not mean Option makes people passive, lazy or complacent. When someone really wants to improve areas of his life or environment, when he sees value in it, he'll acquire the necessary information and knowledge. Honesty saves anyone from spinning his wheels allowing him to concentrate instead on what he really knows he wants.

The Seat of Unhappiness

The seat of unhappiness is ignoring what we want and holding on to the belief we are always "supposed to" or they are always "supposed to". "Supposed to" creates expectations, false hopes, cardboard confidence. It is doing to others what we don't want anyone to do to us, that is, impinge on free choice. "Suppose to" designs and dictates other people's lives, and then lets us choose to feel hurt and confused when the other person opts for something other than our imposed "supposed to".

"Supposed to" really means "You better do what I want or else". "Supposed to" implies a threat you are going to get very upset when you don't get your way with people. "Supposed to" is how we all maintain order and insure predictability for ourselves, which is okay as long as we are aware of how much we are sacrificing in so doing. Option says it's much easier to live naturally, to live free. Why put yourself up for ransom by ignoring what you really want. When you do what you want, you take care of yourself. When you do what others want, without insuring self-value, you tread the quick-sands of unhappiness.

To live naturally is to live free. It is to know exactly what you want. No one owes us anything because we are all free. We are all able to take care of ourselves. We have it all, if we want it. Freedom is a constant, and freedom is what anyone with the Option attitude manifests to all he comes into contact with.

CHAPTER SIX

THE OPTION SESSION AT WORK

We have seen how anyone interested in using Option to help others attains the Option attitude, shares the Option attitude and allows a person who hurts to realize he can have whatever he really wants. It is obvious to the reader the success of Option is attributable to its acceptance of reality, specifically its teaching the only natural laws are those rooted in the very nature of being. The fact a human being is a free being, capable of choice is at the same time a natural law. The fact things are the way they are, and not always the way we'd like them to be, is also a natural law. Agreement with reality is the starting point for Option. Once that agreement is attained and cemented, so to speak, then anyone can make progress in the area of his choice. Without that agreement, helping others comes to a standstill.

Option is not an inexorable approach to helping others. It can be easily learned and applied when one is willing to accept its general principles. Option offers no weighty theories which must be mastered, nor does it require one to discard whatever assumptions have proven of value in the past.

What makes Option ideal for those interested in helping others is its power to meet immediate needs. No one has to scour the past for the causes of today's upset. Immediate resolution may be had in a relatively short time. The Option method admits of no "shoulds or musts". Thus it enables interested people to confront whatever beliefs precipitate inappropriate behavior. The Option method is really a skillfully crafted technique freeing us all to experience the totality of one another and thereby provide immediate attention to the our problems.

Option frees as well any person who hurts. Once one accepts his own freedom, he rejoices in the revelation he does not <u>have to be unhappy anytime.</u> Suddenly, a person who is unhappy realizes what a terrible burden he has been carrying all these years.

People make quick strides through the Option method once they objectively and dispassionately confront their beliefs, because they then allow themselves to direct their energies towards what they really want in life. When one can truly exercise his power of choice on his own behalf, he learns how great it is to feel good once again.

Using the Option method in a situation where you want to help another is quite simple. You do not need to come together in a formal situation. Remember, you are not a therapist, nor are you practicing therapy. You are simply an interested person willing to help another in need. So all you do is allow the person you want to help to state in his own words whatever upset, worry, pain or unhappiness beset him. You may begin by simply asking "How can I help you?" or "Is there anything worrying you today?" or "How do you feel right now?"

While the person tells you his problem or describes his present feelings, refrain from reacting to whatever you see or hear. Without judgment or labeling, <u>receive</u> what is offered to you. Makes no attempt to paraphrase the person's words. Don't caricature in any way the other's problem.

If you do not understand a given point, what then? Option suggests you ask for what is called a "clarification". We talked about this already, remember? In a clarification, you ask for a rephrase or repeat, so you can get the real sense of whatever is being communicated right then. Clarification obviates the need to put words into another's mouth. Clarification is based upon the assumption the person who is hurting is his own best expert. He really knows what bothers him and to what extent and degree.

Clarification is a process enabling you to ask questions in a non-threatening manner so as not to risk your own understanding of the problem being presented. In this way, you protect the other person's freedom and integrity. So if your friend says he feels terrible right now or is unhappy because he and his wife do not communicate, you can refer to the problem without inferring the person you are helping is at fault.

Clarification helps you achieve understanding, prevent distortion or any matching beliefs. When I was young, an old priest used to tell us there were two things people will not abide, namely, advice and a kick in the pants. Clarification helps you keep your observations to yourself but your eyes, ears and intelligence on the other person at all times.

Examples Of The Option Method in Use

Let's examine some examples of the Option method in use. The technique is not to be memorized, of course, since then it would be almost impossible to use. The model questions should be learned, but you want to realize the thrust of your questions depends on your own experience of the person presently with you. Sensitivity and openness will allow you to achieve the greatest advantage for both the person you want to help and yourself. The Option model comprises three basic questions, as we already mentioned

1) WHAT ARE YOU UNHAPPY ABOUT?
Clarify.
2) WHY DOES THAT MAKE YOU UNHAPPY?
Clarify.
3) WHAT ARE YOU AFRAID WOULD HAPPEN WERE YOU NOT UNHAPPY ABOUT THAT?
Clarify.

You realize by now these three questions are simply probes. In and through these questions, you give the other person an opportunity to speak about his choice of unhappiness over happiness in a given situation. The person may tell you in this way why he chooses to be unhappy right now.

The questions are neither judgmental nor condemnatory. Neither are they threatening nor accusatory. They simply permit someone to reassess his present choice and position, so he may discover whether he really does want to be unhappy right now. Perhaps he believes he "should" be unhappy for some reason or other. The questions will uncover his beliefs and his "reasons" to a degree that may prove startling to him.

Following are edited transcripts of actual Option sessions. "O" stands for Option while "C" stands for client.

SESSION I

O   What are you unhappy about?

C   My landlord.

O   Could you be more explicit?

C   My landlord is a real pain in the neck.

O   What you are saying is your landlord is someone you choose to get upset about?

C   No, he makes me upset. That's the problem.

O   Why are you upset about your landlord?

C   He's cheap. He's sneaky. He's unwilling to make any repairs.

O   So it's your judgment your landlord is not a very nice person and he is very difficult to live with or to like?

C   Yes, there's no more ornery person around.

O   I see. But why do you choose to become upset with him. Are you supposed to like him?

C   Wouldn't he get you upset?

O   If I chose to become upset about this person you're speaking of, I'd have my own reasons. What I want to know is why <u>you</u> choose to become upset with him.

C   That's my point. I think it's obvious. Anyone in their right mind would become upset with a person like him.

O   What are you afraid would happen if you were not upset about this person?

C   I'd look stupid. This guy would be walking all over me and I'd let him. I'd be the laughing stock of the whole apartment building.

When I become upset, I put him on notice I wiɪɪ not let my rights be trampled upon.

O   Why does being happy, instead of unhappy, mean you are stupid or wishy washy?

C   It doesn't really, now that you mention it.

O   What do you mean?

C   What I'm saying is being happy is not being stupid. They don't go together. I feel happy a lot of time s but that doesn't mean I'm stupid.

O   What you are saying, and correct me if I am wrong, is you really don't have to be upset about this person. But you do believe, under the circumstances, given how ornery he is and how other people would react in the same situation, you <u>should be unhappy.</u> You really have no other choice. You believe unhappiness is called for and through unhappiness alone can you change an undesirable situation. Is that correct?

C   I guess you could say that.

O   If what I said is true, then look at the burden you put on yourself by choosing to be unhappy, when you do have other options. What is your goal here? What are you attempting to achieve by being unhappy? Is the burden you choose to bear actually helping you attain what you purport to want?

C   Look, all I want is that this landlord get off my back and be nice to me. When this fight is over, I'll be glad. I don't need the aggravation. I have enough problems.

O   Is what you are saying then is you cannot become happy without first becoming unhappy? Isn't that like trying to get something from nothing?

C   Well, I know I have been happy in the past when I thought something good was happening to me. But believe me, this landlord is a real battle ax.

O   Let me ask you a question? If you were happy, would the landlord still bother you?

C   No way.

O   If you were not bothered, would you still be willing to make rational choices for yourself? Would you still want to get what you want? Would you still be able to dislike something without becoming upset over it?

C   Yes. I know I don't like vanilla ice cream, but as I think about it now, I also know that I don't get upset about vanilla ice cream. I also know a happy person makes clearer choices and usually gets what he wants.

O   What are you afraid would happen were you happy in this instance with your landlord?

C   I already told you, it would make me look like a doormat. But as I speak, I also realize when I am happy, I'm not necessarily a doormat. I still want things and I still take care of myself.

O   In this case, were you to <u>choose</u> to be happy, would you be doing what you want, that is, what served you best rather than simply reacting to the ugliness of your landlord?

C   I think I know what you are saying. When I'm upset, I see my landlord as childish, neurotic, mean. I make nasty judgments.

O   And when you are upset, you give away power, don't you? Does the landlord really have the power to make you upset, or is this something you hand over to him?

C   I know what you are saying.

O   No one has a natural power to make another person upset. We choose upset as a means of taking care of ourselves, based upon the belief that in a given situation, there exists no other choice but to be unhappy.

C   Well, I like to win. I like to overcome, to conquer. I'm really a poor loser when it comes down to it. When I don't get what I want, I go crazy.

O   Sounds to me like you <u>need</u> to be liked. You believe you are <u>supposed to</u> like your landlord, so you choose upset because it seems he won't let you like him. What's more, he comes across to you as ugly and not a very nice person.

C   What should I do then?

O   What do <u>you want to do?</u>

C   I just want to be happy. I want more for myself. But life is so hard. So much gets in my way. Not just my landlord, mind you. He's only one of many. I have such a rough time getting what I want.

O   I understand, but if you did what you wanted, would you still have problems?

C   I can't do what I want. That's the problem. I have obligations, things I have to do, places I have to be. I have lots of promises to keep. My time is not really my own.

O   Do you really believe all that?

C   Yes. I can't just sign off from the world with a smile and let everything go to hell. I have responsibilities.

O   What is responsibility?

C   Things one has to get done. I have to pick up a paycheck. I have to feed my family. I have to obey the law. I have to go to church. I have to give good example. I have to love my neighbor and respect my elders, etc. etc. etc.

O   Do you want to do all these things?

C   I have no choice. That's exactly my point. I made commitments and I am a man of my word. My word is my bond. I stand behind what I believe is right.

O   So you are saying you really don't want to do all these things you list, but you have no alternatives, no options. You'd rather be doing other things, and you just go through the motions.

C   Well, when I was young and single, I had more freedom. The older you get, the more you have to conform and toe the line. That's what responsibility is all about. You do your duty, you pay your dues. Later on, you may get to enjoy the fruits of what you presently sow. If you're lucky.

O   Do you like carrying all these burdens now? Is this what you really want?

C   No, if I had money, life would be a lot easier for me. I know I would be a lot happier.

O   Do you really believe that?

C   Yes, I do. I believe without money, life is tough. Money talks. It opens doors. Without money, life becomes almost intolerable, painful, boring. No one respects you when you have no money.

O   That's possible, if you really believe these things. But why do you burden yourself now and postpone living and being happy right now. Do you also believe in your later years, when you are retired and the kids grown, you'll have time for yourself and be able to do what you want?

C   Right now, I'm resigned to life the way it is. I see no escape from my obligations, except to be irresponsible, which I am not and do not ever intend to become.

O   Are you saying you are doing what you are doing now, that is, carrying all those burdens, living in misery and unhappiness so others who need you can be happy? Do you really believe that?

C   Yes, I made promises and I'll be keeping them even if it kills me. That's the only fair and forthright thing to do.

O   What will happen when you die? Will all those people who "needed" you also die when they discover that you are no longer around to give them what they need?

C   I sure hope not. They'll survive some way, of that I am certain.

O   If they'll survive then, why not now?

C   It would not be right to abandon them now. They need me, and as long as I have my health and some money, I can give them what they expect from me.

O   Isn't it true that you need to be needed. You are unhappy when you can't pin yourself onto someone else?

C   What do you mean?

O   Well, you just admitted that without you, those all people who now need you would be able to survive even though you are dead. Yet you also say that they now need you in order to survive. What changes in them when you die and are no longer around. Do they suddenly become more resourceful, more self-sufficient with you out of the way?

C   I see what you mean. I am putting my need on them. I am making them responsible for what is going on in my own life right now.

O   Well, what do you think?

C   You may be right. I never looked at it that way before. Here I am saddled with all these obligations and I am not honestly admitting I do it all for me, because it's what I want to do.

O   Let me ask you a question. Have those people, whom you claim need you, asked you at any time to live your life for them?

C   Of course not. But that's what I want. What I do is what everyone does. That's the way life's supposed to be.

O   There's no natural law, no "it can't be otherwise" that I know of, stating one is supposed to be needed, is there? Can you think of one?

C   No, I can't. But society does dictate the way we all behave.

O   Not that I know of. Everyone is not bound by these laws of which you speak. What you said a short while ago is interesting. You said, "It's what I want". Do you really want to live with all these burdens, living your life for what you believe is "supposed to" be? What about you? What do you want?

C   Are you implying I should dump my responsibilities?

O   I am not saying you <u>should</u> do anything you do not want to do.

C   I don't understand then. What are you saying?

O   I'm saying nothing. I'm simply asking you if you'd rather live your life the way you really want, and be happy? Evidently, all these responsibilities, concerns and "shoulds" are really burdensome to you, and quite unnecessary. But even more than that, they do take a toll on your happiness and health. You really seem to believe, however, things can't be otherwise, when you seek yourself first, you buck natural law. I'm simply asking if it can't be otherwise. Do you want to change and what's stopping you. What are you afraid would happen if you were happy?

C   I don't know. I honestly don't know.

O   Is it because you'd be bad if you did what you wanted and took care of yourself and your own happiness?

C   Yes, that's it. I don't want to be known as a bad person who shucked his responsibilities. That's for sure.

O   What does being "bad" mean to you?

C   Being bad means not being good. It is what hurts or makes you feel bad when you do it.

O   Being bad is doing what other people tell you to do?

C   That's usually being good, if the other people are those who know more than you and always have your best interests at heart.

O   Isn't being bad when you hurt someone, make another person feel bad, or call another bad? Isn't that what you just said?

C   Yes, the bottom line is I don't want to hurt other people or myself.

O   When you feel bad, it means you _are_ bad, right?

C   Yes.

O   You know you can't hurt yourself if you really don't want to.

C   Yes, I know that. But, it's not myself I'm worried about. It's the others. Others can hurt me.

O   But others cannot make you feel bad, unless you say that it's okay with you.

C   I'm afraid I don't understand.

O   If you believe others can make you feel bad, they will do just that. Option says, however, _we_ control our own feelings. We are responsible for what we do and what we allow to happen to us.

C   So what you are saying is I am really in charge. I'm really my own boss. What I say should go.

O   Do you know that to be true? Don't believe it just because I say it. You don't owe me anything. Come to your own conclusions based on what you _know_ to be true for you.

C   Well, I know I can choose to feel good when I want.

O   Try this little exercise. Think of something or someone who "made" you feel bad about ten years ago. Do you still feel bad about that even now?

C   No, of course not. That happened years ago.

O   Yet, you can think about that situation and still not feel bad. Why is that?

C   Because I don't want to feel bad, that's why. It's old stuff. It's just not worth it. It would serve no purpose to become upset about it now.

O   So you can choose to feel good or feel bad, right? It all depends on what you want and your attitude, right?

C   Yes.

This is just a sample of a typical Option session. The Option person touches the present moment in the life of another and is thereby able, with simple, honest questions, to confront some major beliefs behind present behavior. In the session, the other's life is explored in depth, but he is allowed complete freedom to say what he wants, to discuss what he chooses to discuss, when he feels like so doing. There is no script, no ritual, no right way, no wrong way. All this is made possible because Option is really an attitude, a point of view allowing sincere people to relate to reality in the manner most comfortable to both of them.

In the session, the client arrived at some major insights about himself and his behavior. But he did the work. The counselor knew what questions to ask, when to ask them simply because he maintained a non-judgmental attitude. The counselor had no schedule to keep, no points to cover, no syllabus to follow. He was there when another needed him. The counselor did not force-feed any of his own beliefs to the client. Yet the client's beliefs were confronted as they arose in a simple, direct and no nonsense way.

It is difficult to speculate whether the client could have gained the same insights on his own, without the questions and support of the counselor. This much however can be stated, namely, that the Option procedure permitted the client a degree of self-understanding that proved satisfactory and effective. Because the counselor's role was non-intrusive, he was able to help the client see the real self in an engaging and direct fashion.

Let's review another session. Even though these transcripts represent sessions conducted by a professional counselor, that does not mean you cannot learn from them how you, as an ordinary non-professional, sincerely motivated individual can bring help and support to anyone you wish to help. This time, as you read through the text, try to look for the attitude. Let the sequence of questions flow and try to notice there are no "shoulds, musts, have to's" throughout the whole session. All you will find is one human being helping another get in touch with feelings and beliefs and ultimately both achieving self-knowledge and resolution.

SESSION II

O   How can I help you?

C   I don't know. I think I feel all right today.

O   Well, is there anything special you would like to talk about today?

C   I have so many things bothering me I just don't know where to start. I could fill a suitcase with my problems. But right now, I feel okay. I'm trying not to think about myself and my problems right at this moment.

O   Well, just for the fun of it, let's go through one of your "problems" and see if we can help you resolve it. Okay?

C   Sure.

O   Well, which one will it be?

C   Every morning lately, when I get up, I start to feel tense. My chest constricts and I have this sinking feeling in my stomach. It's like butterflies, but a little more angry. I wonder to myself what is going to go wrong today. What fires will I have to put out. I can't look forward to doing what I want, like going on a trip, buying a new car, or getting a present for a friend because I have so little money right now. Business is really off.

O   So business being off makes you feel bad? You have this burden to carry around every day?

C   Yes.

O   Would you like to be free of this morning fever?

C   I sure would. It's all new to me. Just started to happen when the money supply went down. The little bills started to pile up. I have a foreclosure notice on my house. The banks want my car and my ex-wife is threatening to get the police after me because of child support delays.

O   All right. Would you agree that not having money right now, sufficient to take care of your needs, is seemingly the cause of your troubles and pain?

C   Yes sir.

O   What about not having money gets you upset? I assume you do have some money, but not enough to allow yourself to feel free. Is that so?

C   Yes, I do have some money now. Things can only get better. Some day, I expect they will. But right now, I 'm not living as well as I used to. I have had to give up a lot, make a lot of sacrifices.

O   Money and happiness go together for you?

C   Isn't that true for everyone? No one wants to be a loser. My friends don't come around any more. They don't want to hear about my bad luck. In the beginning, they offered help and some were caring. But it's just going on too long for anyone to like it.

O   You believe money brings happiness?

C   I've said it before and I'll say it again: Yes. money talks.

O   Why does not having money make you feel bad?

C   When I don't have the money I want, I feel inhibited. I guess you'd say I feel kind of impotent.

O   What are you afraid would happen if you were without money as you say you are now, yet you were nonetheless happy?

C   No way. One has to be unhappy if he doesn't have enough money. People would say you were crazy, dumb and lazy if you allowed yourself to be happy notwithstanding your money problems.

O   Are you?

C   No. I know I'm none of the above. But I can't control what others will believe about me. All I can do is realize I am expected to behave in a certain way, whether I have money or not.

O   So what you are saying is you know you can't control other people's impressions of you; you know you are not crazy, dumb or lazy; and you live your life nonetheless according to what admittedly you cannot control, namely, other people's ideas and expectations.

C   What I hear you saying is I am contradicting myself. I am also making other people responsible for the way I choose to feel and behave.

O   Are you?

C   Well, the way you put it, I see I'm crazy when I try not to seem crazy for the sake of people I don't even know.

O   Don't look at what I say. Simply ask yourself now if you want to live your life in this uncertainty, worrying about what other people think of you, especially when you know in your heart you cannot control others nor can you do anything about what others think of you.

C   Of course I don't. Yet that is exactly what I seem to be doing, right?

O   Well, what do you want?

C   I want to be happy.

O   Does money make you happy? I mean does money have a natural power within it to make anyone happy who possesses it? Is there something in the nature of money that it is able to act on you, like for example, the sun can tan you because the sun of its nature is a source of heat. Is money similarly a source of happiness for everyone?

C   Of course not. Money is hardly a natural source of happiness. I know a lot of people who have lots of money yet are miserable. But I believe the proper use of money can make you happy. It has a lot to do with the way you live, because in our society, money means everything.

O   Tell me how money makes a person happy.

C   It removes strains and pressures.

O   You seem to put a lot of faith in money. Haven't you just told me you know people who have lots of money and are still unhappy. Do you know any people who don't have much money and are still happy?

C   Yes.

O   Then do you really believe money is in and of itself a natural cause of happiness? Is it like a happiness pill?

C   No, but what counts is what you do with the money.

O   I don't understand.

C   Well money in and of itself is not capable of making you happy, as though it were a magical amulet. But you sure can go a long way with money in your pocket. Without money, forget it.

O   So money depends on what <u>you</u> do with it. You are the ingredient that empowers money, right?

C   Yes. I now see money doesn't have happiness within it, like a milk container contains milk or the acorn, the oak.

O   What does all this mean for you right now?

C   Happiness is inside a person. It is something I can choose. Happiness has to do with me and what is going on within me.

O   Happiness is something we create for ourselves, through responsible choice. Is that something you can agree with?

C   Yes. I see now I've been letting my happiness depend on something inert, inanimate and impotent.

O   Perhaps you also believe if you do not have much money, and are nonetheless happy, you may not try to get more money. Is that so?

C   I don't understand.

O   Do you believe were you happy, despite the fact you had little or no money, you might sit on your laurels and avoid going out to hustle up some more money?

C   Well, in a way. You see, unhappiness has always been my prod. I don't really want to be unhappy. When I am unhappy, I always try to do something that will shake the unhappiness out of me. I used to think money was vital, necessary and essential. So to get out of the doldrums, I get unhappy even more and that pushes me out to make money so I can be happy again.

O   You said it, not me. But now, do you honestly believe you still need a prod or is <u>wanting</u> enough? Do you really believe in order to be happy one must first choose to be unhappy?

C   No, not any more. I used to. But that was because I didn't know what I was believing. I see now what I have been doing to myself. I am always in charge, but for a while there, I was putting money in the driver's seat.

O   You make a very good point about the origin of happiness. You know happiness is always a simple choice, a decision as it were. And being happy is as easy to achieve as breathing. To breathe, you breathe; to be happy, be happy.

C   I see that now. I have been choosing to be unhappy because I believed unhappiness was natural and expected; the way things were supposed to be.

O   Can you see anything unnatural about not having a lot of money, being happy and still wanting more money so you are willing to do whatever it takes, in a responsible way, to get more money?

C   No, that is not unnatural. I can be in a better mental state when I am happy. I can make proper judgments about how and where to get more money when I don't weigh myself down in depression by feeling sorry for myself.

O   And also, you now know that being unhappy can only be unproductive. In other words, is unhappiness helping you right now to earn more money?

C   You are right. I've been poor and unhappy for some time now. Being unhappy hasn't helped one bit to put me on a better road.

O   When you let your decision to be happy depend on anything outside of yourself, what you do is really transfer power. You become like the biblical reed, swaying in the wind. If you are to surrender, then you have to make sure that your external props can deliver, right?

C   Yes, I see what you are saying. I totally agree. I guess I have been believing the wrong things all these years.

O   I wouldn't say what you believed was wrong. It simply was not working for you. Here's how I see what happened. You believed certain things. You acted in accord with those beliefs. You did what you believed in. Everyone does. The problem was your particular beliefs about a particular situation ignored your innate power of free choice. Your beliefs took you outside of yourself in your search for happiness. The result was dissonance between what you did and what you expected as a return on a specific behavior. You thought you were planting string beans, while in fact, you planted cucumbers. Instead of looking at the seed the next time, you persisted in planting cucumbers again and again, thinking they were string beans. You believed the energy and enthusiasm expended in the planting could give you more than what the seed was or what the seed by nature contained.

C   That's a different way of putting it. My energy and effort were doubtlessly wasted. I lacked what it took from the word go. I never had the right seed to begin with for my purposes.

O   Remember, you cannot get happiness from unhappiness. It is like trying to get 1 from o. It never happens.

C   What about beliefs makes them so fickle and untrustworthy?

O   Well, beliefs are once removed from truth itself. They could be true and they could be not true or false. When we blindly accept beliefs as true, we are really trusting the credibility of another person. Simply put, first hand, direct knowledge is closer to the truth than is belief. In fact, first hand knowledge is truth. You can control first hand knowledge, because it is born from your own experience of reality. You know what you know, but you don't know what others know unless they tell you.

The previous session shows how to use the Option questions. The material presented in itself is not important, but the form is. What you learn is by asking the right questions, you can usually coax another person whom you are helping into providing soul searching answers.

The beginning of the session usually starts slowly, but once a rhythm is achieved, the client relaxes and moves forward. He is not afraid to talk about himself and his problems because he knows the counselor will not correct him nor in any way admonish him towards more appropriate behavior. Through the use of the Option method, the client learns he is really the only one who can solve his problems, and by unearthing the beliefs behind his problems he finds the path to resolution.

There is no claim through the presentation of these transcripts a total healing or permanent solution was achieved or not achieved. What is important for you to learn is each time you meet with someone in order to help, you can draw the person out of himself in a non-threatening, productive, effective manner, simply by using the power of the Option method.

Here is another session. Again, we urge you too look to the form, that is, how the questions are presented and what cues the client provides the counselor to prompt a particular question. There is no patter nor pattern to memorize. Simply put, in Option, the counselor experiences the totality of the client, helping him discover his own voice.

SESSION III

O   What are you upset about?

C   Robert.

O   What about Robert upsets you?

C   I wish he would talk more. I wish he were more like other kids his own age.

O   Could you clarify that for me?

C   Well, Robert is four years old. But he's so quiet and withdrawn. He knows a lot and he's very smart. But he keeps to himself. That makes me upset.

O   What about his behavior upsets you?

C   I feel bad for him.

O   Do you believe his not talking as much as you would like is something that is bad?

C   Yes. He doesn't communicate. He'll be hurt later on. People will not treat him right. They'll say he's retarded or some such thing. They'll put labels on him.

O   What about that gets you upset?

C   I think, in fact I know, Robert is a very smart boy. But if he keeps acting this way, others will not know what I know about him.

O   Do you believe things will be difficult for Robert if he does not communicate?

C   Yes. He'll be rebuffed a lot. As a result, he will withdraw even more.

O   But why are you upset about this?

C   I guess I believe others will hurt him. I want better for Robert.

O   You believe two things as I see it. People can hurt Robert and he needs to talk more. Is that correct?

C   Yes.

O   Let's take them one at a time. First, people will hurt Robert. Do you really believe others have the power to make Robert unhappy; that he has to be unhappy if others are wrong about him?

C   No, not really, but he is so young. How does he know to be any better?

O   True, he is young. But he's old enough to want things, isn't he?

C   Yes, that's for sure. He does tell you quite explicitly what he does want. If he wants a certain game, he speaks quite clearly and forcefully. If he wants you to play a particular record for him, he just gets up and tells you.

O   So Robert does know what he wants. Therefore, he doesn't have to be unhappy. That's something you can teach him, right? All you need do is cultivate the right attitude, meaning you show him by your own life one never has to be unhappy. He'll pick that up quite quickly from you, won't he.

C   Yes.

O   The second point is you believe Robert needs to talk more. Let me ask you something. Aren't there times when you don't talk? You just might not feel like saying anything in particular. And then too, there are some people you just never feel like having a conversation with, right?

C   Yes.

O   When you choose not to speak under those circumstances, does that not talking make you unhappy? Does it mean you are mentally retarded?

C   No.

O   You kind of like it, don't you?

C   Yes.

O   Well, Robert is doing the same thing, and for the same reasons you do. He gets some value out of his choice not to talk, not to answer you. It's a way that he takes care of himself, protects himself.

C   I never looked at it that way.

O   What do <u>you</u> want?

C   I want to meet Robert on his own terms, at his values.

O   Right. What you may want to do is find out what interests Robert- bugs, music, singing, whatever. Show him he can get more of what he wants if he talks and answers people. Show him talking is something that can be valuable to him at times.

C   I see what you mean. I have been resisting Robert's behavior. What I want to do is show him I accept him, I love him, despite his choices, regardless of where he is right now. I love him for what he is.

O   What are you afraid would happen if you did not get upset with Robert's failure to communicate to the degree and intensity you deem best.

C   It would seem I didn't care about him.

O   But you do care, don't you?

C   Yes, a lot.

O   So how does being upset make you care more about Robert?

C   I guess it really doesn't. I can see that now. Right now, I'm not sure how I can help Robert.

O   Do you want to help him?

C   Yes, very badly, so much that it often hurts.

O   What do <u>you</u> want to do?

C   I want to help Robert become happy, healthy and smart.

O   He already is all these things. You can improve on each by example. Kids imitate, right? A role model will help Robert. If you see him for what he really is, happy, healthy and smart, not the way others see him or say he is, then you can be happy with him, reach him on his own terms and at his values. Love him for what he is. Do not let him feel you do not approve of him the way he is. When you feel bad around him, then he gets the impression that he is bad, that there is something about him you don't approve of. Love Robert for what he can be, that is, a happier, healthier, smarter little boy.

C   I think I know what you are saying to me.

O   Have you read Barry Kaufman's books, <u>Sonrise</u> and <u>Miracle To Believe In</u>?

C   No, I don't believe so. I saw the TV story, however, where there was a little boy who had some problem. That is what brought me here, in fact.

O   Good. Well I suggest you read those two books. You'll find helping a special child is simply allowing the child to be what he is, and then by providing a loving, supporting environment, you are able to guide the child towards a greater awareness of himself and his world. You won't ever help the child if you think he has to be sent back to the "child factory" as though something is wrong with him. You help the special child when you know he is everything he is <u>supposed</u> to be right now, in this present moment, and with that attitude as a starting point, you are empowered to help the child grow and develop in love and freedom.

SESSION FOUR

O   What are you upset about?

C   Not having anything meaningful to do in my life.

O   What do you mean. Could you clarify that by giving me a specific example?

C   No one needs me, except for piddling things. I used to be a teacher, with all kinds of excitement in my life, a sense of fulfillment even. No more of that.

O   What about that gets you upset?

C   I like to be needed. I need to be wanted.

O   I understand. But you don't get upset about everything you like. You like traveling, good food, companionship, a lot of other things. But do you become upset when you don't have them?

C   No, you're right.

O   So what about not being needed right now gets you upset? As you say, you need to be needed.

C   Yes, I feel I'm supposed to be doing something with my life.

O   Why do you believe that?

C   Everyone is supposed to do good things, especially teachers.

O   What do you mean specifically?

C   People expect teachers to help. A teacher received special training for just that one thing—helping people. He is supposed to go out there and give of himself.

O   Do you believe that?

C   Yes, very definitely.

O   What are you afraid would happen if you didn't get upset when you are not needed?

C   It would mean I'm accepting a state of being useless. I'm not doing what I'm supposed to be doing, and when I allow that to happen without protest, I'm simply saying to myself and to the world it's okay to be lazy.

O   Does being upset and unhappy make everything all right? Does it help you to change and get back on track?

C   Not so far. I sit by myself, but no one gets the message that I'm burning up inside with disgust at my idleness and non-productivity.

O   If being unhappy with your present state is not getting the results you want, and people aren't even aware of the message your unhappiness is supposed to convey, then why continue with it? Why not give being happy a chance. If people notice you are happy, wouldn't they want to be around you more? Who likes a sourpuss, a person who always feels sorry for himself?

C   I see what you mean. But I do find it hard to smile when I know each day is going to be a real drag for me.

O   Have you tried smiling more? It's really your choice whether you are happy or unhappy. It has nothing to do with what is going on out there, but everything to do with what is happening inside of you.

C   But isn't it only natural to choose upset when you do not get what you want?

O   You tell me. Is there any law in nature that so stipulates? Is this like the law of gravity, that is, without exceptions?

C   You lost me there.

O   You never have to choose upset, no matter what. There has to be a reason telling you to choose upset because of value you hope to gain by so doing. Becoming upset is always a choice, a decision you make.

C   I see.

O   Let me put it this way. What are you afraid would happen if you did not become upset?

C   Well, people would think I liked the bad things they do. They would continue using me as a doormat. They wouldn't have any respect for me.

O   Are you telling me that you only get respect when you become upset and unhappy?

C   Let me put it this way. If you make things uncomfortable for people, they stop doing whatever upsets you. It's like a kid and the hot stove. He touches the stove—it burns—and the next time, he is real careful about the stove.

O   That's what upset does for others. Do you like what it does for you?

C   Not really. It doesn't make me feel good, that's for sure. It hurts and I end up feeling lousy.

O   Is this what you want for yourself?

C   No, it's not. But if I don't become upset, how can I protect myself?

O   Be happy!

C   That sounds dumb. Everyone is walking all over you and you react by smiling and being happy? Come on!

O   Does being happy keep you from getting what you want?

C   No, but I don't really see happiness as an effective technique to keep people off your back or to keep them in line.

O   Look at being happy as a way of getting what you want. How do you usually get what you want?

C   I ask for it.

O   And if people do not give you what you want, what happens next?

C   I become upset.

O   With everyone, every time?

C   No, not everyone.

O   How do you decide whom to be angry with?

C   Simple. If I care about the people, or if it's not worth getting upset, where I'll lose rather than gain, then I choose not to become upset.

O   Do you get more of what you want when you become upset?

C   No. I just find more and more people use upset, as I do, to get what they want. It works. So I use it too.

O   What do you mean? Everytime someone gets upset with you, you give them what they want?

C   No, you're right there. But you must admit people use upset to control. They feel they can get you to do what they want that way. If you don't get what you want, then get upset. Getting upset is more manipulation than anything else.

O   What you say may be true. Life is perhaps like that for many people. But a person who believes upset works and uses it a lot to get what he wants, really pays a high price. He is also irresponsible, because he believes upset comes from outside of himself. We know it's impossible for anyone to "make" you upset. You have to want to go along, otherwise any attempt to "make" you upset is futile.

C   Why then does a person become upset?

O   A person becomes upset by choice when he believes he <u>has to</u> because something bad threatens him. He thinks he has no other choices. Furthermore, such a person believes he is a victim unable to do anything <u>but</u> become upset.

C   That's true. I decide when to get upset and when to ignore the whole thing.

O   Let me ask you a question: does it hurt to tell other people what you want?

C   Only if it makes the other person upset, that is, if I think my stating what I want causes him to blow up.

O   Do you believe you have that singular power whereby you can actually "make" another person upset against his will? Doesn't he become upset because he so chooses, and he believes he <u>has to</u> become upset?

C   Yes. I know now I have nothing to do with his becoming upset. It's his choice, his decision.

O   What about another person becoming upset forces you also to choose upset?

C   I sometimes believe it's all a question of self- defense.

O   Why not say you believe the other person's reaction is "bad". And so if he is bad to you, you believe you must feel bad. Bad = Bad.

C   True.

O   If you look at the other person's belief in the inevitability of upset and then take a minute to look at your knowing there is no inevitability in upset, what happens?

C   I don't know.

O   Yes you do. For example, take a person who believes differently than you do, say a man of another religion. He believes that snakes are sacred. Do you necessarily have to take on his beliefs just because he believes in them?

C   No I don't.

O   If you are not Jewish, would you believe a bar-mitzvah is required of all your male children?

C   No.

O   If someone believes he has to be unhappy, why can you not divorce yourself from this belief and look at the person as just holding a belief different from yours? Where does it say you have to believe what everyone else believes?

C   I see what you mean.

O   Do you believe what Muslims believe?

C   No, they have their own religion.

O   How about wearing sheets?

C   I don't believe in doing that.

O   What are we saying?

C   I choose to become upset when I am upset. I don't have to be upset. I know that is true. It's not a belief, it's what I know.

O   What else do you know.

C   I also know I choose my upsets. I only become upset about what I believe is bad for me or those I love.

O   What else do you know?

C   I know people who believe in having to choose upset as an inevitability do not share my beliefs, so when I come across them I can calmly observe them when they live out their belief. I can go about my own business without feeling the need or the urge to convert them or to believe with them.

O   What does that mean?

C   Others have their beliefs. I know what I know.

It is important to realize the foregoing transcripts are but samples of the Option method. They were chosen because they best illustrate the skill of the counselor in eliciting self-knowledge and effective resolution from his client.

At times, the counselor did interject statements into the client's stream of communication. But notice none of the interventions were dogmatic, nor were they anything but an attempt to steer the client towards confronting his beliefs.

The person being helped then, is the key to the Option counseling session. Whenever the person seeks confirmation for a belief from the counselor, the counselor always responds by asking the client "What do you think?" or "What do you want?". By throwing the ball back to the client consistently, the counselor shows what the client already knows but is afraid to admit, namely he (the client) has all the answers to his own problems, if only he would listen to himself, trust himself and give himself a chance.

CHAPTER SEVEN

CURRENT PROBLEMS AND THE USE OF OPTION

S tress, phobias and addictive behavior are quite frequent in our fast-paced society, and for this reason alone, any help you can get from Option in helping your friends, relatives or acquaintances who may manifest such disorders should be welcomed. Of course, you will want to refer them to professional help at all times. However, your concern, help and interest may be the very bridge needed to bring them to the professionals. So don't underestimate your influence in these areas.

<u>Stress or Distress</u>

Stress seems to be a household word today. It confronts us at every turn. Yet in normal dosages, stress is essential. Without it, we would literally collapse never getting anything done because we couldn't overcome physical inertia.

When people complain about stress, they really are referring to "distress", a high degree of agitation leading to unrest, weariness, frustration, tenseness. Physical ailments such as hypertension, strokes, cardiac arrest and even cancer are said to have roots in distress.

Distress is the fruit of inappropriate behavior, whereby one reacts so negatively as to be incapable of meeting present demands. Distress is really another word for anger, resentment, fear, disappointment, frustration, any negative reaction to our environment. Distress is a state of unhappiness whereby a person chooses to become upset by believing a particular person, place or thing is bad or harmful. Thus, he freely chooses unhappiness because of a negative judgment about a particular situation.

Having learned Option, you know, notwithstanding the reasons offered by a person to justify his unhappiness, we all cause our own distress. There is no intrinsic causality between a problem and one's physical environment. One's environment simply mirrors the internal state of the person in the environment.

The scenario for distress is obvious. The stressful person comes into contact with a person, place or thing he does not especially care for. He feels compelled to show his dislike by choosing to be unhappy. To evade responsibility for his choice, the person blames his stress on the disliked person, place or thing.

Not so, says Option. The person, place or thing has no power over anybody. They do not emit magical waves of distress. No human being is a puppet whose strings are pulled by life's changes. He is always free and therefore can choose what he wants and how he wants to feel. Option says stress has its roots in the mind, or one's perception of reality. A cenobite, for example might consider not having money as a blessing, while a man with a low paying job and a family to support would hardly agree.

Whenever a person perceives something other than himself, he makes a decision concomitantly as to whether he will be happy or unhappy about what he has perceived. Since life is a series of choices, the human being always makes decisions freely. Option says behind every decision lies a judgment or belief as to whether what one perceives is considered good or bad. When what is perceived is considered useful or of value, then it becomes desirable. When perceived as bad, hurtful or dangerous to the self, it becomes undesirable.

Many stressful people are actually living out their nursery tales throughout their adult lives. For them, there is always a big bad wolf and a little Red Riding Hood. There are always black hats and white hats, a cruel step-mother and a mistreated, beautiful prince or princess. They keep looking for the knight in shining armor who one day will rescue them from their everyday, humdrum existence. The more they suffer, the unhappier they become, the more they frantically search the skies and horizon, hoping to hear the cavalry call, that moment in time when good triumphs and they are snatched from the jaws of tedium and pain. The sooner a person realizes what havoc he wreaks on himself through fairy-tale vision, the sooner he is able to extricate himself from his stress and get on with the business of being responsibly free.

Option says since distress is under our control, we remain free to confront and change the beliefs leading us to regard our environment as harmful or undesirable. No one has to choose fear, anger or debilitating rage. He can let go of the tremendous burden of distress simply by accepting his own experience of reality rather than the perceptions of second-hand beliefs.

Once the burden of causality is put where it belongs, namely on the unhappy person's shoulders, he achieves a feeling of control. He no longer thinks and acts like a victim. He knows where his distress comes from. He knows to reduce his stress, all he need do is tailor his beliefs to reflect reality rather than altering reality to fit preconceived biases.

Through Option, distress can always be turned around by showing the unhappy person how to take responsibility for his own life, to confront his beliefs and to allow himself to live free.

<u>Treating Phobias</u>

Phobia is another popular malaise. In our day and age, few people will not admit to suffering some phase of this very "in" illness. Phobias can be effectively handled by Option. A phobia is basically an irrational fear expressing itself through paralyzing symptoms, such as shallow breathing, heavy palpitations, sweating, choking sensations and so on. Essentially, a phobia is a judgment something or someone is bad for us.

The object of a phobia can be most anything, but more often

than not, phobias center on cars, driving, snakes, heights, bridges, water, airplanes, elevators and so on. Thus we have claustrophobia, a fear of closed places; agoraphobia, fear of crowds and so on.

What is happening with a phobic? Usually, such a person believes a particular object or behavior is harmful. So a person with a phobia about driving cars believes the car or the highway could get him into a major accident. It could kill him, or someone else could get hit, or someone could hit him from behind, or he could get lost and never find his way home. The phobic sees all the other cars on the highway as menacing, dangerous and bad. When he gets behind the wheel, his fear of all those other cars, his beliefs about them, the road, other drivers etc. culminate in a paroxysm of fear. His survival instincts come to the fore. He says he can't drive, he'd like to, but the very thought paralyzes him.

The same situation develops in a person with a fear of speaking in public. When he gets up on the platform and faces his audience, or even just thinks about doing that, his knees knock, his tongue gets thick, his mouth becomes dry, his brain is like a wet noodle. He can't think of a thing to say. While on the podium, oftentimes he cannot even see his audience. They are like a huge blur to him.

Or take the person with claustrophobia. He will not even enter an elevator. He sweats, grows pale and trembles at the very thought. He could even pass out if forced to remain against his will in any small, tight area. Then there is the young boy who will not go near the water because he is afraid he'll drown. If thrown into the water against his will, he panics and sometimes loses the power to keep himself afloat.

As we all know by now, the belief operating at a basic level in every phobia is the perception a given specific action or behavior threatens one's survival. One feels completely out of control and at the mercy of unseen, hidden forces. What makes the phobia even more crippling is the added belief having a phobia means a person is abnormal, crazy, different from others. Sometimes this shame and embarrassment compounds the phobia and keeps the person so afflicted from seeking professional help.

The traditional technique for treating phobias is the process of desensitization, whereby the phobic is urged to experience, little by little, step by step, through guided imagery, the object or behavior feared. Once the phobic is internally comfortable with his role in terms of the object or behavior, he is helped by former phobics to confront his badman face to face. He thus receives invaluable support in that he knows having a phobia does not equal odd or crazy.

The Option method deals with phobias more directly, since it confronts the beliefs behind the behavior and helps us realize there is nothing on earth truly "bad" or harmful. Option thus allows us to defuse what we believe is a fire breathing monster. Once the beliefs behind the phobia are isolated and confronted, we are in a position to responsibly choose whether we will exchange unreal beliefs for experiential, hands-on knowledge.

Following is an example of how phobias might be treated using the Option method.

O   How can I help you?

C   I think I have a phobia.

O   What does "having a phobia" mean? Can you give me an example?

C   I'm afraid to drive a car.

O   Do you want to drive? Is driving important to you?

C   Yes, very much so. But every time I think about getting behind the wheel, I start cringing, my heart begins to beat wildly, I get a sick feeling in the pit of my stomach and I find my palms start to sweat. I wish it were otherwise. I feel so stupid. I mean, even kids drive today. I'm afraid to drive because I might get lost, someone will hit me from behind, or I'll get killed or permanently maimed or even hurt someone else. I see all these terrible things and feel them whenever I see myself behind the wheel of a car, and so I put off getting my license to drive. The net result is I feel bad because I feel so helpless in this area. This phobia really has me licked.

O   What about driving gets you upset?

C   I just finished telling you. I'm afraid of getting hurt, or hurting someone else or getting hopelessly lost. I have no sense of direction at all. Deep down, I'd really like to drive. I'd like being able to come and go as I please. I wouldn't have to depend on anyone. I wouldn't lead the life of a hermit.

O   What are you afraid would happen if you didn't get upset about driving?

C   I don't get upset on purpose. It's not that I chose this fear or even choose it right now. I'm talking about a phobia, something that takes hold of you and renders you inoperable in a certain area. Newsweek had a whole story about phobias, and believe me, they are more prevalent than we suspect. When this phobia grips me, there's nothing I seem able to do about it.

O   Do you really believe that you are helpless in the face of a phobia?

C   Yes. I can sit in a car that isn't turned on, and I'm okay. I can sit next to someone in the front seat who is driving, and that's okay. But once I am behind the wheel, and there is traffic all around me, forget it. I turn into a bowl of jelly.

O   What about traffic gets you upset? You can ride in traffic, you can walk in traffic, but you can't drive in traffic. What's the difference in your mind?

C   People are crazy on the road. You never know when someone will come out of nowhere and hit you head on. It's really dangerous driving these days. You take your life in your hand. There are too many nuts out there on the road.

O   What are you afraid would happen if you didn't get upset about the traffic and the so-called "nuts out there".

C   I would go out, sit behind the wheel and then maybe get killed or kill someone.

O   So getting upset protects you from the crazy drivers and the insane traffic? It also protects you from hurting others or getting hurt yourself?

C   Not really. I see what you mean. I'm not cool when I'm upset. It would be like a surgeon operating when he's upset. He wouldn't be using all his potential. He couldn't concentrate on helping his patient. He'd be more apt to make a serious error while upset, then when cool or in control.

O   Exactly. But what do you see your upset coming from? Is it really outside of you? You picture driving a car as bad, as though you of all the drivers in the world can be put into a death-dealing proposition simply by getting behind the wheel of a car. You believe you are different than all other drivers because you can hurt yourself and others inevitably, while all other people can drive safely and intelligently. You are actually making a conscious decision to become unhappy about your being such an odd ball.

C   In other words, I consider driving a car a threat to myself and others, as something bad, and then I choose to get upset or scared just to prevent myself from hurting myself?

O   Yes. If driving a car were like going on a vacation, that is, a pleasant and enjoyable experience, would you be unhappy about driving?

C   No. I see what you are saying. But why do I believe that driving is something bad for me and not for others? I know driving is really not per se a bad thing. I will ride in a car if someone else is driving, and his driving is not bad for me. Other people I know drive a car. Some just love to drive. One of my friends tells me driving actually relaxes him. He loves to go on long trips, just him and his car.

O   But you believe driving is bad, and as you say, you go on the road, get in a car even with someone you don't know, like a cab driver, and allow others to drive you or your loved ones in that horrible, hurtful stream of traffic you fear so much. So it's not driving per se that is the real problem, is it? It has more to do with your belief about yourself and driving. That mix is what gets you to choose to become upset with yourself. Perhaps you believe you are not a good driver, one who is capable of handling all the demands of driving. Perhaps you believe you would be dangerous on the road with a wheel in your hands.

C   Yes, now I see that's the real problem—me and the car. As you were talking just then, I was saying to myself "How true!" I just don't believe I have the skills and the knowledge right now to be a good, safe driver.

O   So if you really want to drive, if driving is important to you, what's the next step?

C   I go and do what it takes to become a good, safe driver. I get into a driving course that will give me the feeling I know what I am doing when I am behind that wheel. Only when I'm ready, do I go out on the road.

O   What happened?

C   I see now driving a car is not like being thrown into the water without a paddle. I can go down the road slowly. I don't have to drive in the fast lane. I can always be in control of my speed. I can sign up for a driving course. I don't have to have my license at any specific time or for any specific purpose other than when I want. When I'm ready, I can go and take the driving test. I'm really and have always been in charge.

O   How do you feel about your "phobia" now?

C   I see now what has been going on. It is true that behind every fear lies some kind of imperative. I felt I should have my driver's license, as though having a driver's license was like having an arm. I wasn't listening to what I really wanted. I'm not afraid of driving, but of myself. I know now that I can handle myself. When I think driving now, I think of driving school, not a highway with cars racing and buzzing all around me. I can handle driving now.

This is but a brief example of how Option effectively shifts the emphasis from fear to control allowing a person to take charge of his so-called "phobia". Prior to the session, driving a car was equated with terrible, fearful outcomes. After the session, driving equated with preparation, driving school and ultimate control.

Option effectively removes the coercive dimensions of a phobia, that deadening sense one has to perform or else, that feeling someone is different if he or she does not conform. The person with a phobia is helping to do what he really wants to do. Once his beliefs and fears are effectively confronted, he knows he can always do what he wants.

A driving phobic wants the freedom and independence a driving license can mean; the claustrophobic would rather reach the 27th floor without walking all those stairs; the agoraphobic wants the freedom to buy his own food at the local supermarket. But the means to the desired end is what all phobics find frightening and it is with the means to the end they feel helpless. Option temporarily abstracts from the means and focuses on the goals of the phobic. It shows a person how he can achieve his goals by concentrating on what he can do, on what he really wants to do. So for example, the phobic was able to look at a driving school as a non-threatening "means" of gaining his goals before venturing out alone on the highway.

Option is not one-shot, or short term. In helping phobics, more than one sitting may be required to help the person accept what he is doing to himself, to enable him to realize a phobia is not a free-floating germ attacking people without warning. Option requires patience so you can help the person discover his options.

We mentioned that a phobia is not an entity, a kind of viral infection distinct from the person himself. You want to understand and accept that. Most counseling today accepts the fiction clients are unfairly attacked by such intangible microbes as phobias, alcoholism, obesity, heavy smoking, drug addiction and so on. The emphasis in treatment is on the so-called "disease". In drug addiction, methadone is sometimes provided as a less vicious substitute for heroin, purportedly to wean the client from the more deadly drug. Reality says all the counselor has done in such cases is substitute a less harmful invasive agent.

The "external force" theories in counseling suggest freedom can be vitiated by unknown powers. Option says man is always free. Man does what he wants, and is therefore responsible and accountable. It may serve a person to hear he can shrug off responsibility by blaming "external microbes" but that does not change the real nature of human beings.

This is not to say that Option is hard-nosed about self-control and the proper use of freedom or will power. Rather, Option persons are generally supportive and always helpful, concentrating on the beliefs behind any inappropriate behavior. Option helps a person face up to his behavior and confront his life realistically. Dishonesty about reality simply creates a longer rehabilitation period blocking the road to recovery.

Let's look at alcoholism, for example. Today it is fashionable to refer to alcoholism as a disease, which it may very well be. Such labeling, however, confirms the helplessness of the client. He becomes what he is told he is, namely, a victim. He believes something is happening to him over which he has no control and so he seeks pity, sympathy and absolution. How would an Option person handle alcoholism? Let's see.

O   How can I help you?

C   I have a problem, a real! problem...

O   What is it you are upset about?

C   I am an alcoholic. All I have to do is see liquor and I turn into mush. I can't resist. I have to have a drink even when there is nothing around to drink but water. I get up in the morning and it's two or three martinis right away, even before I even have coffee. For lunch, I have another three or four belts. Then I sleep it off and start all over again at the local bar when I get up. I come home at night, drunk, abusive, hurting all the people I say I love. I've lost my job and most of my friends won't even speak to me. I just can't go on like this.

O   Have you had any kind of therapy or treatment for this?

C   Yes, I've been detoxed a few times. I've been to A.A. I've done the whole clean up trip. My wife and kids threaten to leave me for good. They've had it. Can't say that I blame them. I feel so out of control.

O   You'd like to stop drinking too much?

C   You're kidding! I'd give my right arm to get this monkey off my back.

O   What are you so unhappy about?

C   You must be some kind of comedian. I just told you everything that is bugging me. I hate myself. I hate what I am doing to my family, my friends. Like I already told you, everyone is dumping me. I'm just no good. I'm what you'd call a hopeless case.

O   What about being so-called "hopeless" gets you upset?

C   Well, I just don't like what I'm doing to myself, and what I see I am. Being upset about it all is the only thing I know that will keep me on the wagon.

O   You really believe that?

C   Well, if I were happy doing what I'm doing, wrecking my life, wouldn't it be just cruel, dumb and stupid?

O   Let me ask you. You say you are unhappy now. How is being unhappy helping you get better and achieve what you say you want?

C   It doesn't really. But neither will being happy. People would say that I was heartless. I don't care about them. I like living like a drunken sow.

O   Do you?

C   Of course not. I hate it. It's just not right. But I can't help myself.

O   Would you like to be happy?

C   Yes, that's really why I drink...to escape my troubles, to feel good to get away from it all.

O   Is that all?

C   I like the taste of liquor. It's good. I like the highs, but I detest the lows. Why can't I control myself?

O   Who said you can't control yourself. Where is that written?

C   Oh, I know that line. I dress myself, I drive, I write my name. All that is control. But when it come to liquor, I'm just a patsy. I just can't say no.

O   So as you admit, you can control yourself.

C   Yes, but not in this one area. Just realizing that fact makes me so angry.

O   What about not being able to control your drinking gets you upset?

C   Wouldn't it get you mad too?

O   If so, I'd have my own reasons. We are talking about you right now.

C   I should do better. I know better. But I can't seem to help myself. Alcohol is really stronger than I am.

O   Do you really believe that?

C   No, not really. After all, liquor is liquor. Most people handle it. So it's not liquor's fault. What is there about me that makes me such a weakling?

O   You tell me.

C   It's hard to say. It has nothing to do with liquor, does it? It has everything to do with me. And it's all in my head, right?

O   What do _you_ want?

C   To stop being controlled by liquor. No, to be able to control myself and not need to drink.

O   What are you afraid would happen if you wanted that and yet were not unhappy about getting it or not getting it?

C   My being unhappy or disgusted with myself makes me credible to others. Whoever heard of a happy drunk?

O   What do you mean?

C   I see my unhappiness as something I use to show my family and friends that I am actually trying to do something about my problem. It proves I am not complacent.

O   But has being unhappy really helped you and brought you to a point where you can better your present situation?

C   I see what you are saying. Didn't we just talk about this? You want me to be happy, but I still haven't heard you tell me how being happy about my problem would do me any good?

O   Option is not saying that you should be happy _about_ a problem, but despite the problem. Let me ask you once more, does being unhappy help you in any way whatsoever?

C   No, not at all.

O   When you are happy, don't people like you more? Don't you want better for yourself and for your loved ones?

C   I sure do.

O   Being happy simply means you feel good and feeling good is a choice, a decision you make. You don't need whiskey to feel good. You are your own boss. You can stand back, objectively look at yourself, your life and your loved ones and without unhappiness or rancor, decide what it is that <u>you</u> want.

C   I'd like that.

O   Being happy means you allow yourself your mistakes. You are not your own enemy and so you give yourself permission to be what you are now. But you are not stuck with being a drunk, as you call it. You can change anytime you want and are willing to do what it takes.

C   In other words, I stop fighting this mess. I choose to accept myself for better or for worse? I begin to like myself, sores and all? I am happy with me being me? I'm the best I have right now?

O   That's right. Then you are not trying to prove to others what you know is not true, that you do not really drink too much, that you are not hurting yourself. Such an attitude puts you in a good position to clean up your act

C   You mean others don't like me because I don't like myself?

O   What do you think?

C   I would agree. How could they?

O   We get people to agree with us when we make it worth their while. We have to talk their language, offer them something that is of value to them. We ought to at least use the currency that makes sense to them.

C   I see what you are saying. I'm not anything to be proud of. I'm kind of an embarrassment to them.

O   Do you really believe that?

C   No, I'm not like I seem. But they think I stink.

O   What they think or do, they do for their own reasons. You are free to be what you are and what you want.

C   I feel better now. I don't have to be a drunk, and an unhappy one at that. I don't have to be fearful. I don't want to be a scared drunk, so why do I act as though I have no choices. I can begin simply to do what I really want?

O   And what is that?

C   I want to be happy.

O   Once you honestly admit you don't have to be unhappy, then you can see your options. It's the same way with drinking. You need to drink now in order to be happy. That's what you believe. When you take the power of happiness out of the bottle and put it where it belongs, in yourself, then you are in a position to help yourself and get what you want. Otherwise, you remain trapped and helpless. You have to drink now because you believe you have no other choices.

C What do I do now?

O What do <u>you want </u>to do?

C I really don't know right now. I need time to think this all over.

O You don't have to do anything you don't want to do. We can talk and explore all this further, if you want. For the time being, I suggest you give yourself permission to be happy without needing anything. Believe in yourself for a change, trust yourself. Then next time, we'll see what you really want to do.

In dealing with alcoholism, the Option person does not advocate a one time, instant cure. Habits and beliefs of a lifetime cannot be exchanged overnight. But the counselor did offer the client an opportunity to develop an open attitude, one permitting him to live his own life and make responsible choices. In Option, miracles sometimes happen, and the fact the unhappy person begins to honestly talk about what he really wants, about what's going on in his life can represent a significant advance.

The counselor's attitude during the whole session was based upon the understanding no one has to do anything he doesn't want to do. No one is a victim, no one lives under the gun, unless he wants to. The counselor realizes his client believed otherwise, as do most alcoholics. But the fact he believes he is out of control does not mean he is acted upon without his consent and forced to do what he doesn't want to. The alcoholic realized after the session he abuses liquor because he is trying to force it to make him happy. But alcohol is what <u>he</u> wants. There is no external force outside of him paralyzing his "control" center making him an "alcoholic".

Option shows us how to lead unhappy people towards a knowledge and awareness one does not <u>have to</u> shoulder all those "shoulds, musts and have to's". Anybody is as free as he chooses to be. Anyone can confront any beliefs deluding him into believing he has lost his freedom, control and humanity. The simple awareness of being free is all a person may need at times to propel himself on a path of acceptable, fulfilling and enjoyable behavior.

CHAPTER EIGHT

RELIGIOUS BELIEFS AND OPTION

Many people are reluctant to use the Option Method in their own lives or in helping others under the mistaken impression Option opposes basic beliefs and teachings of organized religion. Some critics honestly contend Option is nothing more than crass humanism. They lament the seeming disregard in Option for man's need to believe in a power greater than himself. Some more scientifically oriented critics of Option claim it is too simplistic. They insist the Option approach cannot produce lasting effects in anybody's life, regardless of what denominational beliefs are held. Others would like to try Option but fear in so doing, they must relinquish a God-concept wherein God is pictured as omnipotent and man totally dependent. Such people feel incapable of doing any good without the constant correction of God's grace and help.

It should be obvious to any reader a person with biases or prejudices against the Option method could not effectively use Option in his life. His bias would prove self-fulfilling. If one believes Option won't work, that it can't work, then it won't. Any closed-minded attitude would be counter-productive.

The fact of the matter is Option requires no beliefs of any kind in order to be an effective instrument of self-fulfillment for ourselves or others. What is necessary, however, is an open, trusting attitude. Option asks anyone helping other people to avoid interposing personal, moral judgments, that he make use of the three questions which comprise the Option technique and trust whomever he is trying to help to provide his own answers.

It has been my own experience in many discussions that any distrust of Option is merely another side of fear. Some people honestly believe when they use Option, they no longer can preserve their own personal beliefs, while others fear once the client gains the Option attitude, he necessarily has to reject organized religion and its belief system. As we shall see in this chapter, such fears are groundless since Option is simply a humane system for helping oneself and others, one that focuses on the human potential God bestowed on man.

A Belief Is A Choice Whereby We Accept Another's Experience

Does Option really demand one abandon cherished beliefs? Can a person still believe in God once he acquires the Option attitude?

What is a belief anyway? A belief is basically any assent given to truth, based upon the credibility or trustworthiness of another. As such, a belief is an indirect pathway to truth. Belief implies another person is more knowledgeable than we in situations outside our own personal experience. We subscribe to a specific religious denomination accepting the authority of its leaders on faith. We believe because authority tells us no divine institution could deceive. We live our lives under the guidance of authority, avoiding sin, embracing virtue as best we can.

Life would be almost impossible without beliefs. The fact is we cannot know everything first hand. It follows we cannot _want_ to know everything first hand. We are required to take someone's word for some things. If we need surgery, we accept the hospital and its surgeons are skilled and competent. We believe this but if we have any doubts, we go elsewhere or ask for an immediate investigation of all medical credentials.

Every time we operate on a belief, however, we do take a risk. We minimize these risks by trying to get as much first hand knowledge as possible. The fact is when we do not have direct, experiential knowledge of a situation, we can be duped or tricked.

Beliefs pale when compared to direct knowledge. When we really know something, no third party interposes itself between us and the reality known. When we exercise our knowing powers, we enjoy the full range of freedom, while in belief, freedom is limited since we don't know all we can know about a situation. I can believe the Church's doctrine on the existence of hell. My decision to believe is not based, however, on the truth or falsity of the reality. If hell is what they claim, I want no part of it. If God is what they say He is, then I want Him as my friend and ally so I can avoid hell and go to heaven when I die.

Some people try to put belief above knowledge. "Blessed are they who have not seen, yet have believed". But knowledge also requires a certain trust, a higher form of trust. In knowing, we trust ourselves. As for belief being superior to knowledge, why is there no belief in heaven? Theology teaches happiness in heaven derives not from seeing as in a "glass darkly", but face to face. We know God in heaven directly, for as St. Paul claims, there the veil of faith is rent in two.

Option does not advocate the abolition, eradication or assumption of any beliefs. Option simply affirms beliefs often cause unhappiness because beliefs make freedom conditional. Option opts for knowing, claiming we can get whatever information we need by ourselves without depending on third parties all the time. We have the answers to our problems within us, and it is there we want to go, rather than settling for second best.

A Return To Self-Trust

The allegations Option undermines one's faith or Option is contrary to religion are not true. Option is not against anything, but rather supports whatever exists. Option asks <u>we believe in ourselves, trust ourselves, listen to ourselves and always love ourselves</u>. Isn't this sound theology, a faithful echo of the Gospel's teachings?

More and more believers today affirm a direct knowledge of

Jesus is superior to any traditional, static belief in His existence and power. Such an awareness is precisely what sparked the charismatic movement among Catholics. This movement stresses a personal, direct experience of Jesus Christ, an experience which purportedly leads to a richer, more fulfilling spiritual life, a more dynamic prayer life and a transcendental relationship both with God and man. Blind faith, it is said, bereft as it was of any direct experience with Jesus, left the believer with crusty, dry, ritualistic formalisms.

Theology teaches man is created in the image and likeness of God, and man mirrors the divine reality through his exercise of intelligence and free will. As God is intelligent and free, so too is his creature, man. To limit the full development and exercise of man's intelligence and freedom would seem to insult God Himself, the creator and giver of life. It would be difficult to imagine a true believer of Christian principles who at the same time refrained from a competent and complete exercise of intelligence and freedom.

Far from rejecting the divine gifts of God to man, any one who uses Option in his own life or to help his neighbor advocates a return to self-trust. He leads another to an acceptance of the self, an acceptance grounded in self-knowledge. By underlining the natural, God-given riches to which we all are heir, the Option person is positioned to help anyone begin to heal any breach among body, mind and spirit.

The Option person can believe anything he wants. All Option asks is he not pass on his own beliefs to the person he tries to help; he not give advice, nor attempt any indoctrination. The Option person never urges another to do one thing rather than another, rather he suggests one find out what he really wants to do. He asks the unhappy person he is helping to consider what beliefs presently being held may be sparking unhappiness. It is the one who accepts the help of Option who evaluates his own beliefs and either reaffirms them or rejects them.

Some critics insist so client-centered an approach in a helping setting is equivalent to handing a three year old a loaded revolver. People must be directed at all times, as well as protected, for man has an innate sense of evil. People need authority figures, they need someone to tell them what to do and when to do it. Critics of Option claim the ordinary person just does not have the expertise, experience, education, training or spiritual grace to make valid judgments about what to believe.

If the professionals within the religious field do not trust their flock, do not consider their fellow believers as adult and capable, then it would seem they do their congregations a disservice. The fact is, when God endowed man with intelligence and freedom, He manifested an infinite trust by that very act. Can men of the cloth deny what God has so trustingly and freely given? Since man is free, he can and will make mistakes, he may not always walk the straight and narrow. But as theology teaches, "abusum non tollat usum"- the abuse does not destroy use's reality.

The Church can be the enthusiastic champion of freedom and choice. Church leaders can trust the faithful, allowing them to become acquainted with their God-given powers of freedom and intelligence. Vatican II made freedom of conscience a vital issue in modern day religion. But legalism still tends to obscure the will of the Council fathers. When laws, with their "shoulds and musts" are tied to the shoulders of the faithful, then the right to live life in a responsible and accountable manner gets short shrift. Any person who doubts the reality and efficacy of freedom would do well to review the exhortations of Vatican II.

Is the Option method a call to a lawless society? Is Option calling for a restrictive society? No, Option simply insists everyday people know what is best for them and no authority has a Divine mandate to separate man from his freedom. Option calls for trust because Option knows human beings have a natural ability to take care of themselves. When we are hungry, we eat. No one tells us when to breathe. When we want anything, we do what it takes to get what we want. Option is not against anything, but is simply the logical extension of sound theology and psychology.

Is Option against organized religion? No. Option allows any clergyman can motivate his flock within the perceptual context of organized religion, but he need not employ threats, restrictions or intimidation to get what he wants. If a particular law within organized religion is of value to a person, Option says emphasize that value but in so doing, always respect the person's freedom of choice.

The Healing Value of Religion

What about original sin? Doesn't original sin taint all mankind? The Option person chooses to emphasize Christian healing, rather than sin and objection. Theology holds man was healed through the death and resurrection of Jesus. Through baptism, each Christian shares in that healing process. Through an acceptance of Christ, we are all regenerated and reborn in the spirit of life, light and truth.

Option encourages the followers of organized religion to capitalize on the healing powers inherent in their respective traditions, linking these with the value and worth of each human person. Option avoids emphasizing the negative aspects of religion, especially those theories limiting a person's freedom.

Option admits many people believe when God redeemed man through the death of Jesus Christ, He thereby manifested a powerful esteem for mankind. By exacting death from His Son, God showed the world the value He placed on one single human person. He was willing to allow the death of His own so man might be redeemed. What does the Cross say about God's appreciation of man's innate value? Can the Option person value his neighbor any less?

Though Option is aware many people often suffer in the use of freedom, it does not conclude freedom is therefore bad and must be restricted. When a person does not succeed, do we help him by closing off his options and his opportunities? The good teacher educates his students by drawing out their natural powers, guiding them in the use of what they already have going for them.

Option holds any disciplinarian and moralistic approach to helping others is hardly rehabilitative because religion is redemptive, rather than punitive. The Church has no mandate to punish anybody, for punishment requires judgment. Christ taught only the Father, who sees the hearts of men, justly judges. Dogmatism is not the only pathway to rehabilitation. Dogmatism infers man cannot be trusted, coercion is the only path to reconciliation and a bland diet of hand-me-down beliefs is religion's sole counseling heritage.

Option is a helping system that trusts the client to know what is best for himself, to answer his own questions and to correct his own attitude towards reality. Even though a person has his own beliefs about sin and reconciliation, he need not feel uneasy about the openness of the Option approach. Option teaches mistakes can be corrected, and as long as we are alive, we always have another chance to better ourselves.

Can a person who is responsibly free, who trusts himself, loves himself, listens to himself, who operates from satisfaction and happiness be a blemish on any church? Moralistic judgments condemning the client for his behavior arise only when someone seeks to control the another, when he wants a dutiful son or daughter for his particular denomination. Does the Body of Christ actually need to control its members in lieu of allowing them the self-fulfillment made possible by God's endowments?

Fear an enlightened, free Christian could be a potential danger to the people of God suggests a lack of trust in the God we purport to honor and serve. The Option method shows a person how to be happy now. Option helps eliminate worry, fear, paranoia, distrust. Through Option, a person can be the best he can be and truly fulfill himself.

Option Is About Truth, Love and Trust

Option teaches a simple pathway to acceptance, peace of mind and resoluteness of spirit. Option is about happiness, freedom, living and being. Isn't this what Jesus was all about? Option is about truth, truth known directly and experienced without the veil of casual belief. Isn't this what Jesus was about? Option is about love, a love non-consuming in its brilliance yet illuminating the exquisite genius of the Creator; a love that freely chooses to serve the Body of Christ as a total person, not from craven posture but power. Isn't this what Jesus was about? He preached the truth and promised the truth would make men free.

Option is about trust. The founder of Option likes to stress this trust becomes mutual once a person takes God at His word.

Look at God's choices, he says. First there was Saul and David. God chose Saul to be King, but Saul resisted, hid and demurred. He didn't trust himself, nor did he trust God's selection. Finally, God ordered Saul to obey, and so Saul became King, but his reign was a disaster. Why? For many reasons no doubt, but principally because he refused to trust himself, even though God initially trusted him.

David on the other hand, trusted God's choice and judgment. Moreover he trusted himself. If God thought David was up to the task of being King, then David knew he was. Even though he would have preferred someone from the House of Saul to be King, David graciously accepted God's call and returned God's trust by ruling kindly, effectively and generously.

Then there was Elizabeth and Mary. Elizabeth was chosen by God to bear a child. Elizabeth didn't trust herself. She considered being pregnant at her age a tremendous joke. Her husband was embarrassed. They didn't believe in themselves nor did they believe God was making a smart move. So even God's trust in them did not bring joy into their lives at that moment.

Mary was a young virgin. She trusted both God and herself. Her acceptance of God's choice in her life is proverbial, showing us that when self trust is present, we are more apt to serve and honor God effectively. When we do not believe in ourselves, of what value is our purported belief in God? For God is our creator, we came forth from His hands. Self trust is always linked with trust in God and vice-versa.

Then there was John and Judas. Both were called by God to assist Him in His ministry among men. Judas didn't trust himself, so he didn't trust in God. John trusted in himself and he went on to become the beloved disciple, achieving great things for God and mankind.

We are told by Scripture God did not leave us orphans. We come well endowed by God for the scenarios of life. Yet so many "believers" tend to gloss over man's God-given endowments, not realizing any disdain or distrust of God's creation is destructive of any relationship with the Creator. If the clergy do not believe man is made in the image and likeness of God, man is the jewel of God's creation, then how can the faithful so believe?

Option Advocates Happiness No Matter What

At this point, it should be more than obvious to the serious reader there can be no possible conflict per se between Option as a helping method and anyone's religious beliefs. In fact, mature and realistic religion stands to gain immensely from those in their ranks adopting the Option attitude. Such people are generally mature, realistic, sensitive, eager to help in any possible way. They are assertive, knowing the right path to reach and attain God is grounded in God's natural law.

Option persons do not look to the Church as owing them anything. They see the Church as a community within which they can express their self-possession in a way that honors the Creator.

The Option person realizes in his emphasis on the God given gift of free choice, he does religion no harm, only good. Option allows him to reach into his own soul and thereby provide a helping hand to his neighbor effectively and humanely.

Christian spirituality teaches there is no such thing as a "sad" saint. Happiness has always been the hallmark of genuine Christianity. The early martyrs went to the lions singing and praising God. Suffering and pain do not spell unhappiness.

Option helps unhappy people by teaching happiness is a matter of choice and attitude. We don't have to wait until we die to be happy. Option says we can be happy now, and as free, human beings, we are always able to choose happiness over unhappiness. This is the power God gave us when He created us in His image and likeness.

Option says we never have to be unhappy. Christ said the same thing in so many words. Christ's entire life, His message was a challenge, a call, an invitation to a life of happiness in His service. Christ trusted fishermen, publicans and sinners because he knew their genuine capabilities. His trust is always rewarded as proven by such names as Peter, Paul, Augustine, Francis, Teresa, to name a few.

Why should the Option person abandon his loyalty to Christ and the religious tradition he professes to serve? Why should he believe when he trusts people, he errs? The Option call to inwardness and self-trust is but an echo of the teaching of Christ that taught the Kingdom is within.

What is the Option creed, then? It states the reality of God's many gifts to man. It reflects God's trust in man whereby he endowed him with intelligence and freedom.

Following is an expression of the Option Creed, one any person interested in fostering growth in himself or others may want to adopt as his own:

The Option Creed

I know there is free will and free choice
I know there is universal goodness
I know myself
I know no person or creature is bad.
I know life is a series of choices.
I know we are all responsible for what we think, say and do
I know personal experience is always genuine.
I know I am the reflection of God Himself.
I know I am my own best expert.
I know truth exists.
I know honesty is for real.
I know we are all free.
I know I can be happy now and forever.
I know people are happy or unhappy by choice.
I know it is unnecessary to be unhappy because no one ever has to be unhappy.
I know no one can hurt me without my permission.
I know I am already in the best place, namely, myself.
I know my heart speaks to me.
I know there are no "supposed to's" except what is.
I know my wants are me.
I know the way to motivate is through the offering of value
I know all behavior is motivated by beliefs.
I know it is more natural to be happy than unhappy
I know I am the best I can be right now!

CONCLUSION

In the preceding pages, we explained the Option Method at great length, because Option can be an incredible aid to anyone seriously considering helping people in distress and who are searching for an effective yet simple approach to the needs of every day people. We did not write this book because of a dearth of effective helping systems, for we know the behavioristic, personalistic or cognitive counseling models usually work. Why then so much time devoted to introducing Option's methods and theories?

Option is not just "another" self-fulfillment or helping system. Option attracts the concerned because of its respect for traditional values. In its practical use of the concept of free will, Option offers anyone interested in helping others, a working system that effectively demonstrates the use of the allied concepts of responsibility, transcendental being and personal happiness in coping with every day problems.

When objectively applied, Option enables ordinary people to work together as a team towards the same goal, that is, mutual happiness. Option equips anyone interested in effectively helping others to do so without the assumption of a host of rites and procedures. In my years as a pastoral counselor, I have effectively used behavioral modalities as well as some of the more current counseling procedures. However, since I discovered the Option method and used it in my counseling ministry, I can honestly affirm, with Option, one is able, in a few short sessions, to achieve a degree and extent of problem resolution that often proves startling.

Option gained national attention in recent years as a growth process when the award winning television special "SONRISE" aired over one of the major networks. "SONRISE" told the story of how two people, who had been trained in the Option method, used this very program in treating their own little boy, diagnosed as classically autistic. With the Option attitude, the Kaufmans successfully brought their son, Raun, from the darkness of autism to the light of normalcy, so much so that years later, Raun successfully attends school and relates normally with his environment. The father and mother of Raun, Barry and Suzie Kaufman share their Option attitude with other parents similarly grieved and have established a center in Sheffield, Massachusetts where they train professionals and parents in the use of the Option method. Barry has also written several excellent books about Option, notably "To Love Is To Be Happy With" and "A Miracle To Believe In".

Option vs. Limits

When I was in Thailand a few years ago, I noticed in the southern part of that country, people still used oxen to cultivate and irrigate their fields. Yoked by the shoulders, the oxen kept digging ruts or going around aimlessly in circles. Their shoulders were burdened in such a way controlled direction was easily maintained, either rut or circle, depending on the farmer's requirements. What kept the oxen in harness was the yoke, a little corrective device. Remove that and the animals were as free as they could be.

People today often feel they are either in a rut, condemned to do colorless, boring things that get them nowhere or they are just going around in circles, never achieving what they really want in life. Option helps a person discover what yoke keeps him feeling that way. Option says men are not oxen, that nature designed us all so any time we so desire, we can reconstruct our lives, discover our yokes, and by lifting them, set ourselves free.

Man's yoke generally is the "should". Option says "Get those 'shoulds' off your shoulders" and allow yourself to do what you really want, instead of what you feel you must. Perhaps it would be worth while to review some of the basic tenets of the Option method so concerned people might appreciate how freeing a person can feel once useless yokes are discarded.

Basic Option Principles

Option insists, as its very name suggests, freedom is not an abstract characteristic of the human person. Rather, freedom is a genuine right, a distinct possibility at all times and in all places. We never have to do anything we do not want to do, except when natural law such as the law of gravity, the law of death etc. so dictates. When it comes to human behavior. We always have options.

The reality of freedom makes men responsible and accountable. No one can do anything to you without your permission. By the same token, no one is forced to act for us or against us. When we permit people to act against us. we bear the responsibility. We may not like what happens to us, but we never have to be unhappy about it.

Option also teaches behavior results from beliefs. We do what we believe in and what we believe to be right, apt, effective and self-serving. Our beliefs are judgments about reality as we perceive it. We concur with universal beliefs because we accept the belief-maker is credible, useful or of some advantage to us. So even our beliefs are the object of choice and freedom.

Option states every human being was created to be happy and we can in actual fact, be happy all the time, no matter what. Happiness is a choice and consists of feeling good, at peace, calm.

Option is non-judgmental, humble and loving. Option accepts each person where he presently is, complete with all beliefs and barriers.

Option insists no one can change anyone else. The Option person never attempts to <u>change</u> those who seek his help. He leaves that decision to the one he is trying to help.

Option teaches each of us is always really in control. We are always doing what we want, and we have what we want, even though we are often reluctant to admit this. Option says if you seek to learn what a person wants, just look at what he has. We do the best we can with what we know, and we are constantly trying to take care of ourselves.

An effective Option person is one who has time to look, to see, and to hear the person whom he is helping. Option trains anyone to do just that, because Option hones peoples' observational skills. With the Option training, one avoid being judgmental, always trying to find the right answer, the right word so as to subtly coerce another.

Option says observation begins in the heart. First you have a feeling, then you observe to gain data on the feeling's reality by

<u>being with</u> both body and words. False observation attributes reasons without educing evidence. True observation implies listening, seeing, supporting and refraining from judging or labeling.

Any person trying to understand the Option method so he can effectively use it in helping others or in his own life, might simplify it all by realizing Option is all about helping people choose happiness over unhappiness. When a person sheds his "shoulds", he discovers all the Options God allows. At that point, he can choose to be happy no matter what. That is what the Option method is all about.

If the reader would like more information on current training programs in the Option method, he can write me, care of the publisher. I can state the founder of Option is willing to train people individually, helping them acquire the skills of Option for use in both their personal lives and to make other peoples' lives more satisfying. Barry Kaufman also offers some intensive workshops and programs on the various possibilities of the Option method. You may write to him directly at the Option Institute and Fellowship in Sheffield, Massachusetts.

EPILOGUE

I had just finished leading a six-week training program where a group of about 20 people, from all walks of life, trained themselves to help others. They were a happy group, eager as well to get started. Chuck raised his hand when I asked for further questions. "How do we get started? I mean, where do we go from here?" Everyone laughed good-naturedly. It was a good question, and one always popping up at the end of my training sessions.

No doubt you too want an answer to the same question. You want to know how to get involved as quickly as possible.

When you are happy, you don't have to look for "work". It looks for you. All around you, in your immediate families, in your circle of friends and acquaintances, on the job, at the office or even on the train, there are unhappy people or people who really believe that given something they don't like or want, they have no other choice but to be unhappy about it all. But now, you know differently. You really know you always have options, choices and your whole life is a series of choices. So if a person really wants to be happy, then he just becomes happy. And it doesn't take much to be happy, just as it doesn't take much effort to breathe. You just breathe and so too, you just choose to be happy. Anyone who is alive can do that.

I like to ask my new friends in Option to avoid some pitfalls, and then I give them some practical suggestions as to how they can become involved in helping others on a regular basis.

a) Pitfalls To Avoid

1. Being a know-it-all. When you own Option, it can be a trip. Which is what you don't want. You want Option to be your life, whereby you exercise your options in a responsible, caring manner. That means you don't want to tell Aunt Jenny what her problems are. She knows what they are. I remember Carol. She was a delightful, intelligent, energetic bundle of fun. She told me after she finished the six week training program on helping others, she ran home and started to make a list of all the people whom she felt could use her help. Naturally, her mother topped the list. When she met mother at

breakfast the next morning, Carol proceeded to "help" her mother. Without so much as a "good morning", Carol asked her mother "How can I help you?" Her mother, a good sport, smiled and said, "You could begin by cleaning up your room, then doing the dishes from last night". "No", Carol said with a trace of disappointment in her voice, "I mean with whatever is bothering you right now. Trust me, mother, I know what I'm doing." With that, her mother laughed out loud, and remarked, "You're what's bothering me right now, little girl. By the way, don't you have anything else to do but torment me so early in the morning?" Guess what? Carol stood up in a huff, stormed out of the kitchen remarking in a loud voice, "Well, I guess some people don't even know when they could use some help."

Carol was angry, unhappy, cynical, judgmental — you name it. She told me she couldn't understand why her mother was so complacent about her own happiness. Why didn't she want to be happy? Carol felt mom sure could use a song in her heart. Carol thought she knew more than her mother about what was good for her mother. That may have been true, but trying to take a superior position to her mother was incorrect. Carol had learned a lot at the seminar, and she sincerely wanted to share with her mother. The resistance she met shocked her, because she believed everyone wants to be happy, and if she could help someone become happy, wow, that would be just great. I asked Carol, "Given your mother's apparent rejection of your offer to help her, why do you feel you have to be unhappy?". Carol told me she offered a gift and the gift was spurned or ridiculed. "Given that's what really happened", I smiled, "what are you afraid would happen if you didn't become unhappy?" Then Carol laughed softly. "I guess I believed my mother didn't love me, if she rejected my gifts. Love me, love my dog." "Does your mother love you?", I asked. "Yes, I know she does" Carol replied. "Does your not getting what you want from your mother mean your mother no longer loves you?" Carol didn't answer. It all clicked and in a flash, she knew what had happened.

You know a lot of unhappy people. You'll meet lots more. You'll want to help them because you know you are on to something in the knowledge no one has to be unhappy no matter what is going on their lives. A "know it all" attitude is not what will help you create opportunities to share what you have learned about Option. What should you do? There is nothing you should do. Rather, the question is "What do you want to do?" If you really want to help others become happier, you want to do what it takes. And one thing it doesn't take is a supercilious attitude. As we saw with Carol, that attitude can be a shaking boomerang. We'll review in a while some opportunities for helping you may want to explore. But in the meantime, remember although happiness is contagious, you cannot force your choice upon others. That's what freedom is all about!

What Carol saw in her mother was not a person allowed to be what she wanted to be. Rather she labeled her mother as "imperfect", "having something wrong with her", "defective" as it were. Her mother does not "need" Option. Her mother might want to look into Option at some time in her life especially when she discovers for herself that unhappiness is not the natural, easy, alive way to go. But that will be her decision when the time comes. Carol helps her mother when she allows her mother to be what she wants to be. She is not responsible for her mother because Carol does not make the choices in her mother's life. Her mother is responsible for her own life.

2. Being judgmental. Many times a person notes another is unhappy as Carol did with her mother. How to help them? There seems to a vicious circle here, a catch-22. You have been specially trained to help others, and yet you are also told to let people be, allow them their choices. It's as though you have bought a saw without teeth, all this study and introspection for naught.

Ah, but you know that isn't true. Option begins with you, just as "helping" others begins with "helping" yourself. A person can't help others become well until he goes to school for a specialty, such as medicine, psychology, nursing etc. So too, you can't be of service to those in need until you put your own house in order. That's just the way Option works, because Option is about taking responsibility for your own life and your own choices. To label a person as alcoholic, depressed, strange, cruel, moody, "way out" and so on is really to make a judgment about that person and his choices. A judgment is not something real, as we have said before. A judgment exists in the mind, and it could be true and it could be false, depending on the authenticity of the evidence purportedly giving rise to the judgment. Often enough, a judgment is simply a conclusion, a belief carved in stone by the person himself.

Let me make it clear. The motive for helping another can only come from the person wanting help. Help cannot be imposed and Option does not advocate labeling people and then putting a "Help Needed" sign on them. Option does not come out of judgment, but out of knowledge.

Where does that leave you? As we have observed, there are diplomatic ways of offering help, getting people to look at their lives, helping people to consider whether more happiness in their lives might prove more satisfying than a daily dose of the "glums". One way is to ask questions. But Carol did that, didn't she? Yes, however she came on very strong to her mother, insinuating her mother "needed help". Ask questions about the person, rather than questions that insinuate judgment or put-downs. For example, the simple questions "How are things going?" or "How are you feeling" or "Is there anything I can do for you right now" often lead the other party to talk about themselves or at least create a rapport that might lead somewhere positive.

3   Being a non-listener. People like to talk about themselves, what they've done and in the course of a conversation, open up a lot of themselves. As a trained Option person, you want to listen. Tom was a good listener. He took one of the "Helping Others" seminar and later on, he told me about his dad. Tom could never listen to dad, because dad knew everything, as Tom told it. A conversation with dad was a one-way street. He did all the talking, so the only salvation was the "tune-out" which Tom admitted he did a lot. Tom's dad seemed to hate everybody, distrust everybody, so when he spoke, Tom heard pure and simple diatribe. A commercial would come on TV and dear old dad would pick it to shreds, bombastically observing

how Madison Avenue continued to insult his intelligence. Dad would watch the news and all his racial biases would come to the fore. "They deserved it" or "What do they want, a free ride" and on and on it went for the hour the news stayed on. Dirty liberals, commie pinkos, cruddy press people rode side by side with racial slurs and epithets.

After Tom made Option his own, he decided to listen to dad, and of course, he heard his father's unhappiness. Dad believed he was right and "they" were wrong. Dad believed you had to fight, to get angry, to protect yourself, to be loyal—all the things that made America great, as he put it. But now Tom was really listening. He no longer tuned out. His father became his teacher in Option. Tom used to believe his father could "make" him (Tom) upset. Whenever he began to become upset, Tom would stop and ask himself "Do I really 'want' to become upset about this right now?" and he thereby took responsibility for his choices and feelings.

At first, Tom admitted, it was sheer torture sitting with his father and just listening to him. He said it was quite a 'hat trick' to stand in mud and not get a speck on himself. But it was only when he did not see his father's "speaking" as "mud", as "tripe" as "venom", but as just his dad's choices, that he was able to get beyond personal judgments and actually "hear" his dad.

Tom did not concur with his father's judgments by any means. But the strange thing was his father never asked him to agree with him. His father believed he had to keep on talking, judging, cursing and swearing at people. And that's what he did.

Before long, Tom's dad noticed he and his son were getting closer. Tom was happy being around his dad, and his dad appreciated that. Instead of arguing with his dad, trying to "set him straight", attempting to "educate the bigot", Tom used his energy just to "be with" his dad. He would get his dad a match, he would get him another beer, he would be as nice and pleasant with him as he wanted, and yet avoid any tendency to patronize.

Soon the diatribes lessened in frequency and vigor. Tom's dad started to talk about himself, instead of "those bums, creeps and

idiots" out there. Tom learned things about his dad he never realized
before. His dad was frightened, insecure, afraid of dying. Tom and his
dad talked about these things, sometimes way into the night. Tom
talked about Option, about being happy no matter what, and his
dad listened and learned. It took time, said Tom, but he was able to
help his dad confront a lot of silly beliefs and in the process, his dad
decided energy spent on happiness was more efficient. There was no
instant "conversion" to Option. There was no prosyletizing on Tom's
part. All Tom did was "allow" his dad his choices, take responsibility
for what he wanted and what he himself chose, and stay happy. It was
then his father "changed".

The French have a saying that "the more things change, the
more they remain the same". Option persons know they cannot
change people, which is what many people do not understand. For
most, the word "helping" is a code word for "changing". Carol claimed
she wanted to "help" her mother, but she really wanted to "change"
her. Tom thought before Option his dad was beyond help, but he
meant "change". You get out of the clutches of the catch-22 cited
above when you ask yourself whether your understanding of the
word "helping others" isn't really another way of saying "changing
others". Are you saying others are not all right the way they are and
the way they choose to be? Are you trying to impose your values
upon others? Are you unhappy with the way others live their lives?
Do you "need" others to agree with you? Do you come to others
complete with conditions, expectations and judgments?

A happy person is a nice person, a concerned person, a
sensitive person. It is by being "happy" with yourself, allowing
what is happening with others that you yourself become a helping
instrument. Happiness always begins at home. Tom was patient,
understanding, willing to please because he was happy within himself.
He did not accept being happy gave him the right to make demands
on others or to intrude in their lives without invitation. Tom wanted
more for his dad, and through patience, he got more. Carol also
wanted more for her mother, but she wanted it all right away. She
was unwilling at first to do what was required. She conditioned her

own happiness on her successfully changing her mother's life around. She "needed" her mother to "need" her. When her mother exercised her freedom, Carol became upset. See how tricky it can be? Carol refused to allow her mother to use the very freedom Carol claimed was the essence of the Option method.

There are other pitfalls you want to avoid, such as "needing to make a lot of progress in Option", "needing to be always on a 'peak experience'", "needing to be an Option 'missionary'", "needing to avoid complacency", and so on. Get the equivalent of "pitfall"? It is "needing", that state when we condition our personal happiness on always getting what we want, as though wanting were not enough. The key is to examine your beliefs and see if you won't be happy "unless and until". Then you know you have a pitfall and you also know what you may want to do about it all. Use the three questions. Get on the phone and talk with another Option person and confront the belief behind the unhappiness. If you are unable to talk to a friend, then get out a piece of paper and pencil and write out your answers to the three questions. Find out what you are afraid would happen if you were not unhappy right now. You'll find out why you are not "choosing" to be happy and you might want to do something about that.

A lot of people ask me how I heard about Option and how I got so involved in it. Well, it really is a long story. But it all started when I learned somebody I loved very dearly was diagnosed as being secondarily autistic. To me that was a label at the time fraught with pain, suffering and overall unhappiness. He was a little boy, barely three years old and here he was labeled and cut off from any meaningful future. That was my belief at the time. I heard about the Kaufmans and their work with autistic children, so I persuaded the parents of the little boy to contact them. Unfortunately, the Kaufmans were out of the country and wouldn't be back for some time. So I found out I already knew the founder and creator of Option. In fact, I had taken some training from him previously. I made an appointment with him and asked him quite directly, "How come the Kaufmans used Option successfully with their boy and I couldn't with Michael?" The man answered simply "Well, they did what it took and you didn't". "What was that?" I asked impatiently. "Well" said he, "they used Option. You didn't. They were happy about Raun. You look at Michael as a 'broken doll' and your reaction is to send him back to the factory and get fixed. In other words, for the Kaufmans, there was nothing 'wrong' with Raun. For you, there is something 'wrong', 'bad', 'unsettling' about Michael's condition. It's all a question of attitude."

The man knew I wanted help, so he asked me how he could help me and thus began my odyssey into Option, learning happiness is a choice, happiness is not a goal, but a present state, and giving Michael permission to be the way he was, giving myself permission to be the way I was. I was able to honestly say I loved Michael the way he was, and I could allow him to be the way he was. I was not out to "change" Michael, but I simply "wanted" more for him. The Option attitude was quite freeing, so much so I was able not only to accept Michael, but to actually help him, in the sense of not burdening him with my own "need" to be happy through him.

To give you an idea of what Option allowed me to do with Michael, how it opened up possibilities for me, I'd like to share the following piece I did for Michael one Christmas.

<u>To Michael- Age 7</u>
little boy of blond,
blue eyed angel,
where have you gone?
we need to know your ripples
are really stepping stones
to health and happiness.
elfin, sprite, sunshine,
pained soul within?
whimpers and whispers,
a boy of love.
are you calling out for help?
is your clapping and wailing
and meaningless laughter

but a broken mirror
once shattered in infancy
and now another flickering
where we can see ourselves
and the hurts we may have
heaped upon you?
Come out wherever you are,
we hear you and we love you.
punishments and threats and
pressures are no pathways.
where have you gone and
yet you are always there.
your dancing hands hold the
key to health and happiness.
let us take your hand and enter
your world, crystalline beauty,
so fragile, so open and yet
so closed. No one child with
so much natural richness should
walk alone in confusion and fear.
He should know that his reaching
will be rewarded and that those
who love him will risk with him.
Michael, age 7, going on 8
we will always be there and one
day, together we will all
dance in the sunshine as well
as the rain.

When I wrote that piece, I was crying. I was unhappy about
Michael and yet I was ambivalent. I was happy about Michael
because he was such a happy person himself. I discovered when I was
happy, Michael was a joy to be with. When I was unhappy, Michael
closed off from me and pulled into himself. I knew from my Option
training, an attitude of accepting and loving Michael just the way

he was represented a sure pathway towards helping him. Now I can say Michael does not need me in order to be happy. I can affirm also Michael is happy most of the time. Little by little, slowly but surely, Michael is coming out of himself. Because of Option, Michael experiences a new Springtime, a resurrection, a rebirth every day. To celebrate that, I wrote the following piece the next year at Christmas time. I'd like to share it also with you, because I feel it reflects the fruits of Option, both for Michael and for myself.

A CELEBRATION OF MICHAEL'S SPRINGTIME

The years go on fragile and unrelenting
But the once little boy stands taller.
It's springtime in Michael!

His mischievous smiles are more frequent
As he nudges a once closed door ajar.
It's springtime in Michael!

Deep blue eyes, that oft lacked luster
Now sparkle, darken and shine
In boyish chagrin and virgin delight.
It's springtime in Michael!

What we knew was there all along
Slowly and measuredly is bursting its cocoon.
It's springtime in Michael!

His words in warmth and sunshine
Suffuse our very being and in a
Beauteous ring, hide an innate wisdom;
Assuring us he never really went away.
Once there was winter's cold silence,
But now it's springtime in Michael!

Michael, why is just being with you,
On your terms, so satisfying, so enriching
If not because you really never stopped
Giving and growing- an eternal spring.
It's springtime in Michael!

We notice and we pleasure in the
Daily revelations you permit, happy
You bring us your smile, your singing,
Your skipping, your likes and dislikes,
Your hugs, your kisses, your writing, your
reading, your music, your dancing,
even your screaming and your clapping,
your pouting and your tears,
all signs of growth, aliveness and impishness.
It's springtime in Michael!

We shall never give up as daily we
Fuel the fires of love and acceptance.
We made our mistakes, we failed you
In our quest for appropriateness.
Yet despite our fumbling, you now choose
To share yourself in generosity not
Just forgiving, but healing and saving.
It's springtime in Michael!

Take what time you need, little man.
After all, it's your springtime.
We trust as you trusted all through
The dark bleakness of our attitudinal winter.
At least we now know
It's springtime in Michael!

Push what you will through our cold earth.
Nurture it, guard it, feed it, as
You will. Let your soul grow at its pace.
Let us but bask in the warmth of your growth.
It's springtime in Michael!

Open any door whenever you choose, for
Opened or closed, we see no door, only
A brilliant, blinding, beautiful boy who
From the beginning, even in his silence,
Spoke from the depth of his being
The eloquence of love.
It's springtime in Michael!

When you are ready, our arms remain yours
Our hearts burst in your springtime.
The years roll on, fragile and unrelenting,
Yet we'll salute each new dawn as the once
Little boy grows taller and more willing to
Let us be his world as he is ours.
It's springtime in Michael!

May it always be springtime in Michael!
Praised be God and Michael too!

-Patrick J. Berkery, Ph.D.

I could share with you many other wonderful facets of my life in Option, but suffice it to say, for the present, I am able to help many people who have difficulty being happy despite whatever life hands them. I work with families who have autistic children, I work with autistic children themselves and thanks to the Option attitude, I am able to allow them to be the way they are. From such a premise of acceptance and love, there is little difficulty in wanting more for both parents and children and in doing whatever is necessary to make wanting a reality. With the Option attitude, wanting is always enough.

b) In concluding, I would like to share with you other ways you can become involved in helping people, something we referred to at the beginning of this chapter. I suggest to you a word you may find unsettling at first, but given the Option attitude, you will come to regard as really an opportunity. That word is "volunteerism".

If you pick up the Yellow Pages of your city or town, you will find a section that lists Social Service Organizations, Clubs, Health Agencies, Human Service Organizations and Senior Citizens' Service Organizations or Religious Agencies as well as local hospitals and churches. All of these hurt for serious, dedicated assistance. Or you could contact chaplains at the correctional institutes, many of whom would be delighted to allow you to help them. Following is a list I compiled of human service organizations, most of whom have a place for you, especially if you come to them with the generosity, sensitivity and concern of a happy person.

-American Cancer Society
-American Red Cross
-Birthright
-Catholic Charities
-Catholic Family and Community Service
-Child Care Council
-Coalition For Children & Youth
-Local Community Council
-Association for Children With Learning Disabilities
-State Department of Social Services
-FISH
-Local Family & Children's Aid
-Family Life Center
-Good Shepherd House
-Heart Association
-Info Line
-Local Inter-Faith Community Services
-Local Jewish Federation

-Leukemia Society of America
-Local Child Guidance Center
-Multiple Sclerosis Society
-Open Line
-Rape Crisis Service
-Salvation Army
-Save the Children Federation
-Senior Services Coordinating Council
-Shelter Services for Abused Women
-Cerebral Palsy Association
-United Way
-Local Voluntary Action Center
-Local Hospices
-Local Nursing Homes
-Local & State Correctional Institutions
-Probation Office for Juvenile Offenders
-Local Child Abuse Shelters
-Foster Homes & Adoption Services

We want all the best for you, so you may not only be happy, but you will also want to share your happiness with others, thereby enriching the lives of those you love and all of us who dwell beneath the stars. Helping others is not only an opportunity, but a privilege, for when we open the hearts of others to their own magnificence and uniqueness, we lend exhilarating dimensions to the reality of "brotherly" love. For by this shall all men know we are His, if we have love (acceptance) for one another by sharing our own happiness.

GO FOR IT!

ABOUT THE AUTHOR

Father Pat Berkery is presently in charge of St. Anthony's Parish, in Ansonia, Connecticut. Born in Brooklyn, New York, he contracted polio at a very young age and was treated in and received his grade school education at St. Charles Hospital, in Port Jefferson, New York. The nuns who cared for him did such a wonderful job that he was able to enter the seminary later in life and pursue college and graduate studies in a Connecticut catholic seminary. After ordination, Father Pat was sent to Rome to obtain his Doctorate in Philosophy. While there, he majored in Scholastic Philosophy, and upon completion of his doctoral studies, returned to teach in the Connecticut seminary where he prepared for the priesthood. Father Pat has taught philosophy in various seminaries throughout the country and has written extensively on the spiritual life. He has also preached retreats in many parts of the United States. A published author, Father Pat has written many articles that were published in various religious journals in addition to his books. A gifted speaker and homilist, Father Pat has found that stories have a power to make most messages meaningful and absorbable beyond man's wildest dreams. This is why his latest book *God Helps Those Who Help: A Training Guide To Helping Others* comes at a time in his life when he feels he must share the secrets of genuine happiness.

ABOUT GREATUNPUBLISHED.COM

greatunpublished.com is a website that exists to serve writers
and readers, and remove some of the
commercial barriers between them. When you purchase
a greatunpublished.com title, whether you receive it in
electronic form or in a paperback volume or as a signed
copy of the author's manuscript, you can be assured that the
author is receiving a majority of the post-production revenue.
Writers who join greatunpublished.com
support the site and its marketing efforts with a per-title fee,
and a portion of the site's share of profits are
channeled into literacy programs.

So by purchasing this title from greatunpublished.com, you
are helping to revolutionize the publishing industry for the
benefit of writers and readers.
And for this we thank you.